CW00644542

IRISH RAILWAYS

LOCOMOTIVES, MULTIPLE UNITS & TRAMS

FOURTH EDITION

The complete guide to all Locomotives and Multiple Units, Coaching Stock & Trams of Irish Rail, Northern Ireland Railways & Dublin Trams (Luas)

Robert Pritchard

Published by Platform 5 Publishing Ltd., 52 Broadfield Road, Sheffield S8 0XJ, England.

Printed in England by The Amadeus Press, Cleckheaton, West Yorkshire.

ISBN 978 1 909431 46 1

Above: The new southbound platform at Limerick Junction was brought into use in August 2019. Work is nearing completion on the new platform and footbridge in the background in this view as 220 powers away from the station with the 11.00 Dublin Heuston–Cork on 22 April 2019. **Finbarr O'Neill**

Front Cover photograph: DART EMUs 8120+8134+8105 have just left Seapoint working the 16.05 Bray–Malahide on 11 September 2019. **Robert Pritchard**

Back Cover photograph (top): Enterprise-liveried 8209 passes City Hospital on the last leg of its journey operating the 09.30 Dublin Connolly–Belfast Lanyon Place on 14 September 2019.
Robert Pritchard

Back Cover photograph (bottom): Luas Green Line tram 5009 crosses the William Dargan Bridge on the approach to the Dundrum stop with a service for Brides Glen on 11 September 2019.
Robert Pritchard

CONTENTS

FOREWORD

Welcome to the fourth edition of the Platform 5 guide to the railways of Ireland. This book, although smaller than the other Platform 5 European handbooks, contains a wealth of information about the locomotives, multiple units, coaching stock and trams that operate in the Republic of Ireland and Northern Ireland. We also include details of preserved locomotives and railcars and preserved coaching stock used on the main line.

It has been almost seven years since the previous edition of this book and in that time there have been many changes to the Irish economy and Ireland's railways. However, the Irish Rail and Northern Ireland Railways fleets have stabilised somewhat after all of the new rolling stock introduced during the late 2000s. Changes have mainly been connected with the reforming of the InterCity Railcar fleet on Irish Rail, the disposal of most of the remaining Mark 3s, the establishment of the Belmond "Grand Hibernian" luxury train – for which we have a new dedicated section – and the delivery of additional and longer trains for Dublin's Luas light rail network.

As this book was being prepared in spring 2020 Ireland, like most of the rest of the world, was hit by the coronavirus Covid-19 pandemic. The country closed its borders and "locked down", with train services heavily cut. Two routes, Limerick–Ballybrophy via Nenagh and Limerick Junction–Waterford, temporarily lost their rail service. By the summer the service was starting to get back towards normal levels, with a full service in operation on the DART electric system around Dublin. Many regional routes were still operating at a reduced service, however, some at around half the normal frequency. In line with Government guidance, wearing a face covering was mandatory on public transport from 29 June, but with an "essential travel only" request in place, almost all trains were very quiet with few passengers. Northern Ireland Railways was similarly running a reduced timetable and face coverings were mandated from 10 July. In line with other state bodies Irish Rail and Northern Ireland Railways were receiving government support to continue operating during this time.

For the purposes of this book we refer to the pre-coronavirus timetables, which hopefully should be back in place later in 2020. Notwithstanding the hit to passenger numbers caused by Covid-19, the future of the railways in Ireland looks bright. In 2019 passenger numbers increased for the seventh year in a row, reaching 50 million for the first time in the company's history – an increase of 4.2% compared to 2018. Ireland was one of the countries worst hit by the banking crisis and passenger numbers dropped by as much as 10% in the late 2000s. In 2012 and 2013 passenger numbers were at 36.7 million, but have since grown by more than 36% over six years. In Northern Ireland, NIR carried 15.8 million passengers in 2018–19, again the highest in its history and an increase of 11.3% over two years (and with no additional rolling stock).

For the first time in several years, new rolling stock is now on order for both the north and south – all intermediate vehicles to augment existing DMUs. For Irish Rail 41 vehicles are on order to lengthen some of the 22000 Class ICRs, with another complex reforming programme during 2021–22 set to see a reduction in the number of 3- and 4-cars planned and the return to some fixed 6-car sets. For NIR things will be more straightforward, seven of the 3-car 4000 Class units will be lengthened to 6-car sets, using 21 new cars on order.

A trip to the "Emerald Isle" is always a very enjoyable experience and it remains one of the most popular destinations for British enthusiasts to visit. The InterCity Railcars are excellent trains, and far superior (at least in your author's opinion) to many similar trains in Britain. There are also still plenty of loco-hauled trains to be savoured on the main lines, and most of the trains between Dublin and Cork are once again loco-hauled. The excellent tram system in Dublin has again been extended, and the two lines now finally connect with each other! The preservation scene has also seen some interesting developments and whilst many sites only have a fairly short running line, extensions are planned. Covering the history of the railways in the whole of Ireland, the superb museum at Cultra, near Belfast, is always worth a visit. Railtours are run across Irish Rail and NIR, mainly by the Railway Preservation Society of Ireland (RPSI).

Our monthly magazines **Today's Railway's Europe and Today's Railways UK** give regular news of railway developments in Britain and Ireland: see the advertisement on the inside cover of this book or visit the Platform 5 website www.platform5.com.

This book is updated to information received by July 2020. I would like to thank the following for their assistance in the preparation of this book: Joanne Bissett and Neil Dinnen of Irish Rail, Richard Noble of Northern Ireland Railways, Nigel Farebrother and Finbarr O'Neill. Also the Irish Railway Record Society for hosting an excellent programme of London meetings, which are very useful to keep up to date with the latest developments on Ireland's railways. The IRRS journal is also always a good source of Irish news past and present.

If readers notice any inaccuracies in this book, or have any general comments that may enhance future editions, please contact Robert Pritchard on 0114 2552625 or e-mail robert.pritchard@platform5.com.

Robert Pritchard. July 2020

THE REPUBLIC OF IRELAND & NORTHERN IRELAND

In the early years of the last century there was a movement towards Home Rule in Ireland, then part of the United Kingdom. Home Rule for Ireland had been passed by the Westminster Parliament in 1914, but implementation was shelved upon the outbreak of World War I. Matters came to a head in 1916 when a rebellion was staged against British rule led by Patrick Pearse and James Connolly. The Easter Rising, as it became known, was put down, but the decision of the British to execute several of the leaders for treason alienated public opinion. In the 1918 general election Sinn Féin ("ourselves alone") defeated the Irish Parliamentary Party and constituted themselves as the first Dáil, or independent parliament, in Dublin. The British attempt to smash Sinn Féin led to the War of Independence of 1919–21. In December 1921 an Anglo-Irish treaty was signed and 26 counties gained independence as the Irish Free State. The last constitutional links with the United Kingdom were severed in 1948 when the Republic of Ireland Act was passed.

Six of the Ulster counties preferred to remain in the United Kingdom, becoming Northern Ireland, and were granted their own parliament in Belfast in 1920. This was later dissolved in favour of direct rule from Westminster, although the devolved Government was restored for a time and then dissolved again. It has now been restored thanks to agreement between Loyalist and Nationalist politicians.

A Note on the Irish language

Article 8 of the Constitution of the Republic of Ireland states that "The Irish language as the national language is the first official language". However, only approximately 55 000 people out of a total population of around 4.5 million are estimated to be native Irish speakers and these tend to be concentrated in small discontinuous regions, mainly around the western seaboard known as the Gaeltacht. Nevertheless, Irish schoolchildren spend 11 years learning the language and the names of public bodies are all written in Irish first. Thus, Irish Rail is known as Iarnród Éireann, Irish Bus as Bus Éireann and Dublin Bus as Bus Atha Cliath. In normal conversation the English names are invariably used (except for Bus Éireann) and as this book is written in English the name "Irish Rail" and abbreviation IR is used throughout.

▲ 8103 was returned to traffic in 2018. On 10 September 2019 two different types of DART stock pass at Raheny. On the left 8510/8520 Class Japanese DARTs 8629/30 and 8614/13 form the 11.20 Howth–Bray as 8103 arrives leading 8102 and 8118 on the 10.35 Bray–Howth. **Robert Pritchard**

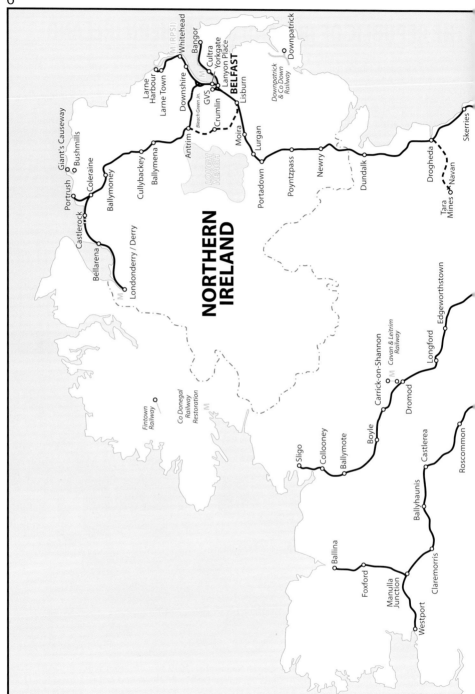

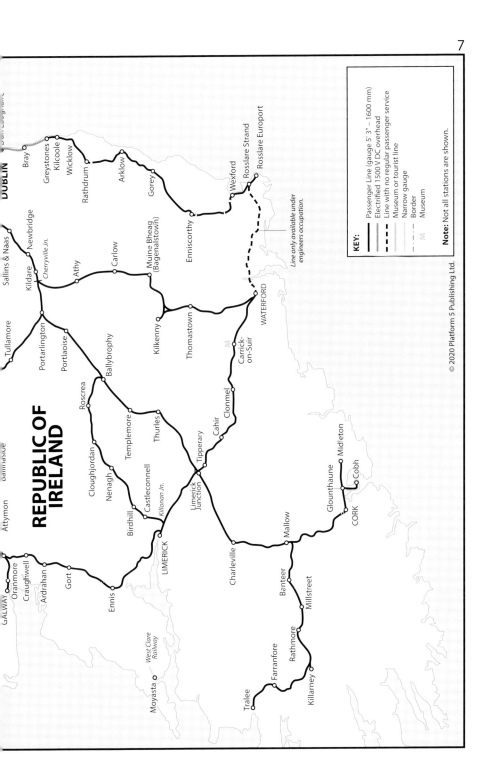

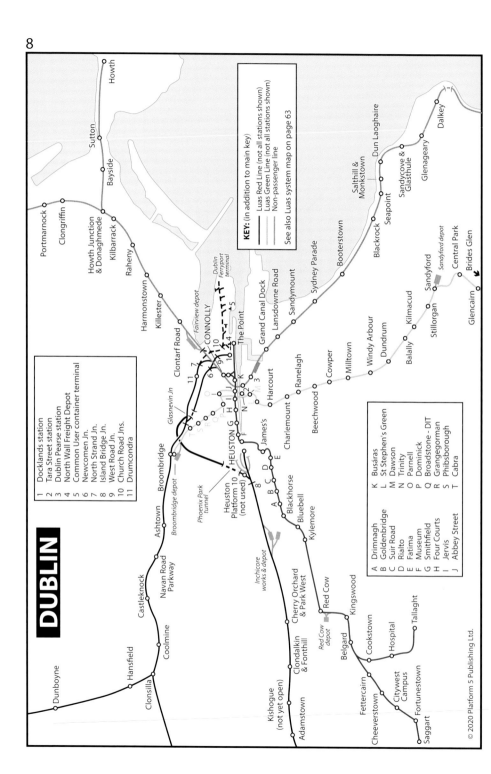

DUBLIN

KEY: (in addition to main key)
— Luas Red Line (not all stations shown)
— Luas Green Line (not all stations shown)
— Non-passenger line

See also Luas system map on page 63

1 Docklands station
2 Tara Street station
3 Dublin Pearse station
4 North Wall Freight Depot
5 Common User container terminal
6 Newcomen Jn.
7 North Strand Jn.
8 Island Bridge Jn.
9 West Road Jn.
10 Church Road Jns.
11 Drumcondra

A Drimnagh
B Goldenbridge
C Suir Road
D Rialto
E Fatima
F Museum
G Smithfield
H Four Courts
I Jervis
J Abbey Street
K Busáras
L St Stephen's Green
M Dawson
N Trinity
O Parnell
P Dominick
Q Broadstone - DIT
R Grangegorman
S Phibsborough
T Cabra

© 2020 Platform 5 Publishing Ltd.

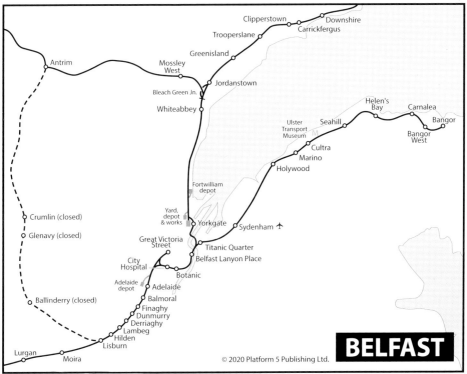

Clipperstown
Downshire
Carrickfergus
Trooperslane
Greenisland
Antrim
Mossley West
Jordanstown
Bleach Green Jn.
Whiteabbey
Helen's Bay
Carnalea
Ulster Transport Museum
Seahill
Bangor
Bangor West
Cultra
Marino
Holywood
Fortwilliam depot
Yard, depot & works
Crumlin (closed)
Yorkgate
Sydenham
Glenavy (closed)
Great Victoria Street
Titanic Quarter
City Hospital
Belfast Lanyon Place
Botanic
Adelaide depot
Adelaide
Balmoral
Ballinderry (closed)
Finaghy
Dunmurry
Derriaghy
Lambeg
Hilden
Lisburn
Lurgan
Moira

© 2020 Platform 5 Publishing Ltd.

BELFAST

▲ Belfast Central station was renamed Belfast Lanyon Place in 2018, more accurately reflecting its location, and that fact that Great Victoria Street is much closer to the city centre. On 14 September 2019 4011 leaves with the 16.25 Larne Harbour–Belfast GVS. **Robert Pritchard**

THE RAILWAYS OF IRELAND

The main line railway network of Ireland was built to 5 ft 3 in (1600 mm) gauge rather than the British standard 4 ft 8½ in gauge. There were also a large number of 3 ft 0 in (914 mm) gauge lines which were quite separate from each other.

The five main companies existing before World War II were as follows:

(1) The Great Southern Railways (GSR)

In 1924 the **Midland Great Western Railway of Ireland** (generally known to Irishmen as the "Midland" but having no connection with the English Midland Railway), which owned the lines from Dublin Broadstone to the west and north-west of the country, the **Great Southern & Western Railway**, which owned the lines from Dublin Kingsbridge (now Heuston) to the south and west of the country and the **Cork, Brandon & South Coast Railway**, which owned the lines from Cork City to the south and west of County Cork amalgamated to form the **Great Southern Railway**. The following year saw the amalgamation of the **Great Southern Railway** and the **Dublin & South Eastern Railway** which owned the lines from Dublin Westland Row (now Pearse) and Harcourt Street (closed but since partly reopened as the "Luas" light rail Green Line) to the south-east of the country, to form the **Great Southern Railways**. The GSR absorbed a further 23 minor railways, thereby bringing all railways operating entirely within the Irish Free State under the control of one company.

(2) The Great Northern Railway of Ireland (GNR(I))

This owned the line from Dublin Amiens Street (now Connolly) to Belfast Great Victoria Street and those from Dundalk and Portadown to Londonderry (also referred to as Derry) Foyle Road.

(3) The LMS Northern Counties Committee (NCC)

The lines from Belfast York Road to Londonderry and Larne were owned by the **Belfast & Northern Counties Railway**. This was taken over by the Midland Railway of England in 1903 and operated by its "Northern Counties Committee". This later became part of the **London Midland & Scottish Railway** (LMS).

(4) The Belfast & County Down Railway (B&CDR)

This railway owned the lines from Belfast to Bangor and other points south east of Belfast.

(5) The Sligo, Leitrim & Northern Counties Railway (SL&NCR)

This railway ran from Carrignagat Junction near Collooney, 5½ miles south of Sligo, to Enniskillin.

After the war, in 1945, Coras Iompair Éireann (Irish Transport Company) was formed to run all public transport in the Irish Republic and took over the Great Southern Railways. It was nationalised in 1950. Iarnród Éireann (Irish Rail) was established on 2 February 1987 as one of the three CIÉ rail and bus operating subsidiary companies. Meanwhile in 1948, when the railways in Great Britain were nationalised, the Ulster Transport Authority (UTA) was established to operate all road and rail services in Northern Ireland, taking over the B&CDR in that year and the NCC in 1949. The UTA was disbanded in 1966 with the railways becoming Northern Ireland Railways (NIR) in 1967. However, 1995 saw the reamalgamation of rail and bus companies, although the former is still operating as Northern Ireland Railways. NIR, Ulsterbus and Metro (Belfast city buses) all now come under the Translink name – this is the brand name of Northern Ireland Transport Holding Company which provides public transport in the region.

The GNR(I) remained independent until 1953 when it was purchased by both the Irish and Northern Irish Governments for £4.5 million and the Great Northern Railway Board established which ran the company until 1958 when it was dissolved and its assets divided between the CIÉ and UTA. The SL&NCR remained independent until 1957 when it closed.

The lines from Wexford and Waterford to Rosslare are not owned by Irish Rail. They were built for the Fishguard & Rosslare Railways & Harbours Company and are now jointly owned by CIÉ and Stena Line, although operated by Irish Rail.

Ireland had a large number of narrow gauge railways all of which were built to 3 ft gauge. These were:

The Ballycastle Railway	The Cavan & Leitrim Railway
The Ballymena, Cushendall & Redbay Railway	The Clogher Valley Railway
The Ballymena & Larne Railway	The Cork, Blackrock & Passage Railway
The Bessbrook & Newry Tramway	The Cork and Muskerry Light Railway
The Castlederg & Victoria Bridge Tramway	The County Donegal Railways Joint Committee

The Giant's Causeway Tramway	The Schull & Skibbereen Light Railway
The Londonderry & Lough Swilly Railway	The Tralee & Dingle Light Railway
The Portstewart Tramway	The West Clare Railway

All are now long-closed, but preserved vehicles remain from some of these railways. In addition, preservation societies have restored sections of the Cavan & Leitrim, County Donegal, Giant's Causeway Tramway and West Clare systems to working order.

THE NETWORK TODAY

Most lines in Ireland are single track and most stations have crossing loops. The Dublin–Cork and Dublin–Belfast main lines are double track as is the branch to Howth, the line from Cork to Cobh, the Dublin–Rosslare line as far as Bray and the section of the Dublin–Sligo line as far as Maynooth. There are also short double-track sections between Limerick and Killonan Junction. The eight miles between Cherry Orchard and Hazelhatch & Celbridge was quadrupled in 2009–10 to accommodate an enhanced local service as well as the more frequent service on the main line into Dublin Heuston. At the same time most of the local stations were rebuilt and some resited.

In Northern Ireland the whole of the line to Bangor is double track, and there is also double track section used by Londonderry and Larne line trains between Yorkgate and Bleach Green Junction. The double track continues a short way on the Londonderry Line to Monkstown and on the Larne line to Downshire. All other lines on the NIR network are single track.

All lines are operated only by diesels, apart from the DART area commuter lines around Dublin which are electrified at 1500 V DC overhead.

▲ 2602/01+2604/03 stand in one of the bay platforms at Cork on 13 September 2019 with the 16.40 local service to Cobh. **Robert Pritchard**

RECENT DEVELOPMENTS AND LOOKING TO THE FUTURE

There have been some significant developments in Ireland since the previous edition of this book was published. One of the most important has been the orders for new rolling stock – both in terms of firm orders and future prospective orders to cover the planned expansion of the DART electric network. With the Irish economy now growing strongly once again, both Irish Rail and Northern Ireland Railways recorded their highest ever passenger numbers in 2019 – Irish Rail carried a landmark 50 million passengers.

In October 2019 it was finally confirmed that the long-awaited order for 41 additional ICR (22000 Class) vehicles, representing €150 million investment, had been approved and these would be delivered to cope with the significant increase in demand for peak hour travel into Dublin. Delivery is expected from late 2021 with the lengthened sets appearing in service from 2022. The return to some fixed 6-car sets will enable trains currently formed of 2 x 3-cars to be replaced by fixed 6-car formations, with the 3-cars being deployed for strengthening elsewhere. The current fleet of ICRs were introduced between 2008 and 2012, meaning at the time that Ireland had one of the youngest train fleets in Europe. They were very well received, but there followed a hiatus in orders. Work on a 3-year refurbishment programme for the existing fleet of ICRs also commenced in 2018 and is being carried out in Connolly Valeting Plant.

The fleet is also now more intensively diagrammed, in 2016 just 75% of the ICR fleet was diagrammed, but that has now risen to 87%. The whole of the operational fleet is now committed, a 10-minute DART service was introduced in September 2018 with all trains except one formed as 6- or 8-cars. Most of the Dublin–Cork trains are once again loco-hauled Mark 4 sets – when passenger numbers dropped away ICRs were used on many trains as an economy measure.

On top of the 41 extra ICR vehicles Irish Rail had investigated acquiring redundant stock from the UK and a reguaging programme – Class 170s and 185s had particularly being mentioned, but that has not come to fruition. Also not likely to be taken forward are refurbishment plans for the withdrawn 2700 Class units. Estimates to refurbish the class were much more costly than had been hoped.

Looking further ahead exciting plans are taking shape to expand the Dublin DART electric network. This is due to take part in three stages: Connolly–Maynooth/M3 Parkway, Malahide–Drogheda and then Heuston–Hazelhatch, including a tunnel linking the Kildare line west of Heuston station to the Northern line east of Connolly station (with stations at Inchicore, Heuston, Christchurch, St Stephens Green, Pearse and Docklands) and the completion of four-tracking of the line between Inchicore and Park West (the main line is currently four tracks for eight miles between Park West and Hazelhatch). Work is expected to be completed between 2024 and 2027, with the total budget of €2.2 billion, with €600 million allocated for a new fleet and €100M for a new depot. The new depot is likely to be near Maynooth, with the existing cramped facility at Fairview downgraded to use as a stabling location only. Drogheda would also become an EMU depot, with released DMUs (29000s) transferring to Cork or working services over diesel only lines as 8-cars.

A framework arrangement is preferred for the new fleet as part of four orders, for 480–600 cars, formed as fixed 4- or 8-car sets with some also capable of battery operation as "BEMUs". Irish Rail has said that it will not buy another pure diesel train, future orders being electric only, electric/battery hybrid, diesel/electric hybrid or diesel/battery. Irish Rail, supported by the National Transport Authority, commenced the tender process to order the largest fleet in its history in May 2019, with the first part of the order being for 150 vehicles. The estimated DART fleet procurement timeline is as follows:

Order 1: 150 cars BEMU/bi-mode 2019–23;
Order 2: 100 cars BEMU/bi-mode 2023–25;
Order 3: 150 cars EMU 2025–27;
Order 4: 80 cars EMU 2029–31.

It is hoped that the first trains will enter service from 2024. The final order in the table would be to replace the original 8100 Class 2-car DARTs, which by 2031 would be 50 years old.

Meanwhile, in another project aimed to ease congestion in the capital, a north–south Dublin MetroLink line (previously called the Metro North project) is also being developed as a single line metro from the estuary on the north side of the city via the Airport, one of the busiest in Europe not to be rail connected, and St Stephens Green to Sandyford (Luas tram tracks between Charlemont and Sandyford would be taken over by the Metro). It is hoped that work can start in 2021 for completion in 2027.

On the existing network there have been relatively few developments to report, compared to in our previous edition where a number of new lines had just reopened (the Galway–Limerick Western Rail Corridor, M3 Parkway and the Midleton branch). A significant new service did start in November 2016, following a €13.7 million project to upgrade the Phoenix Park Tunnel line. This allowed some services from the Kildare line to "turn left" just before Heuston and run directly to either Connolly or Grand Canal Dock.

The first services to operate over this line were initially peak time only trains. In December 2018 the service was increased to operate all day, Mondays–Fridays only. At the same time the off-peak frequency was increased on the Maynooth line. In September 2018 a new, much simpler, 10-minute service on DART was also introduced.

One further significant infrastructure development has been the construction of a second through platform at Limerick Junction, significantly improving the layout here. This opened in August 2019.

The Enterprise stock saw a major refurbishment that was completed in 2016. This was a shared project with Northern Ireland Railways – NIR completing most of the work on the carriages in Belfast and Irish Rail the overhauls of the 201 Class locomotives at Inchicore. This work gave the trains at least another 10–15 years life and has been well-received by the travelling public.

Meanwhile, Irish Rail completed its extensive rebuilding of the 18-strong 1976-built 071 Class in 2018 – all locos were fitted with new cabs and heaters as part of the work and despite being more than 40 years old these rugged and reliable locos still play an important part on freight and infrastructure trains. Plans to heavily rebuild the 201 Class locos, using long-stored and fire damaged 230 as a testbed, have been put on the back burner for now. Three bids were received for the work but none were compliant. Instead, some work will be carried out in-house at Inchicore, with an auxiliary power unit to be fitted along with an automatic shut down system to generate fuel savings. The computer system will also be upgraded.

Another interesting development with Irish Rail's two locomotive classes was in October 2019 when an RPSI railtour saw 071 and 201 Class locos (078+232) operating in multiple for the first time ever. The "Cobh Rambler" celebrated the arrival of the first 201 Class loco in Ireland 25 years before.

Irish Rail has been keen to test new technology. One ICR, unit 22007, was fitted with ZF "Ecoworld" mechanical transmission in 2019 as a trial. This generated a minimum 15% fuel saving compared to the current Voith hydraulic transmission as well as more rapid acceleration and the 41 additional vehicles will be fitted with the ZF gearbox (22007 was converted back to standard after the trial was completed). Meanwhile, hybrid MTU power packs are also going to be fitted to some vehicles, which could provide up to 33% fuel savings. The whole fleet could be converted at its half life overhaul.

Resignalling meant that the last remaining semaphore signals around Cork disappeared in 2018, but there are still pockets where semaphores can be seen – around Waterford, on the Limerick Junction–Waterford and Limerick–Ballybrophy lines and on the freight only line at Navan. As part of the route modernisation all automatic half-barrier level crossings and most of the manually operated crossings and accommodation crossings were eliminated, remaining crossings being CCTV operated and controlled from new control and signalling centres at Dublin, Athlone or Mallow.

In Northern Ireland there have been fewer changes. The 3000 and 4000 Class DMUs have settled down well to give a reliable service, and passenger numbers increased to 15.8 million in 2018–19, with no change to the fleet and little change to the service. This meant that several peak hour trains are now significantly overcrowded.

In December 2018 NIR exercised an option to order for a further 21 DMU vehicles, for delivery in 2021–22. These will be inserted into seven of the 3-car 4000s to make fixed 6-car sets. Originally it was planned to augment units 4001–07, but shortly before this book was published the plan was changed to 4014–20. This will give an overall fleet of seven 6-cars and 36 3-cars. More platform extensions are underway to accommodate 6-car trains. More new trains could be purchased in the near future, with discussions around possibly lengthening the remaining 4000s to 6-cars or instead ordering eight new 6-car sets.

The second phase of upgrades to the Londonderry line took place in 2016, with a crossing loop and 6-car platforms in place at the rebuilt station at Ballarena. This meant an hourly service from Belfast to Londonderry was possible. In October 2019, in Derry itself, services were diverted into the former Belfast & Northern Counties Railway Waterside station, the Grade B listed Waterside station has been converted as a centrepiece of the new north west transport hub. The uninspiring and unpopular 1980 station is being demolished and the space will be reused as a bus turning circle and car park. Meanwhile, the rebuild of Portrush station was completed in 2019 and Belfast Central was renamed as Lanyon Place in 2018. Plans are in place, and Translink has been granted planning permission, to rebuild Belfast Great Victoria Street station, as part of a £208 million new multi-modal transport hub alongside the existing station on the site of the former freight yard at Grosvenor Road. Enterprise trains would be diverted from Lanyon Place to the new GVS station.

TRAINS IN IRELAND

PASSENGER ACCOMMODATION

Train services in the Irish Republic are mainly Standard Class and most are Standard Class only. Some trains, including the Dublin–Belfast "Enterprise", most trains on the Dublin–Cork and Dublin–Tralee routes also have First Class.

Dublin suburban services are operated by EMUs on the DART (Dublin Area Rapid Transit) service between Howth/Malahide and Greystones and by Railcars on other routes; all are Standard Class only.

In Northern Ireland all internal services are Standard Class only.

TRAIN HEATING

Only the 201 Class locomotives have train heating equipment. They have an electric train supply built-in for the standard Irish Rail voltage. This is known as "Head End Power" – an American term. On the Dublin–Cork loco-hauled (Mark 4) trains the purpose-built generator car provides train supply so the Head End Power (HEP) is not required. On the Enterprise service the 201s were used to supply HEP but this often resulted in failures, led to excessive noise at stations and also shortened the life of engine components such as water pumps. Locomotives had to be frequently rotated between duties as the GM engines were not designed for continuous use at high revs. Overhauled Mark 3 generator cars introduced in 2012 mean that HEP by the 201 locomotive is not now required.

TRAIN MAINTENANCE

The main works of Irish Rail is at Inchicore, Dublin where there is also a running shed and a large yard used to store redundant stock. Whilst the Irish Rail network is now Railcar dominated Inchicore still has a role in the maintenance of the remaining locomotives and also overhauls bogies for all vehicles. Inchicore is situated about two miles west of Heuston station on the south side of the line.

The large fleet of 22000 Class InterCity Railcars are maintained at a new purpose-built depot around a mile south of Portlaoise, officially called Laois Traincare Depot. The Dublin area 29000 Class suburban Railcars are maintained at Drogheda depot (opened in 2004), which also carries out servicing of the Connolly outbased 22000s. DART EMUs are maintained at Fairview depot, one mile north of Connolly station. There are also stabling sheds at Connolly and Heuston stations which can carry out minor repairs. The 2600 and 2800 Class Railcars are maintained at Limerick, where a wagon repair depot is also located. The depot at Cork generally only carries out minor servicing and refuelling on the 2600 Class units and the 22000s used on the Tralee line.

For a relatively small system, Northern Ireland Railways surprisingly boasts three depots in Belfast. The main facility where the Enterprise coaches and locomotive fleet are maintained is at York Road. A new depot opened in 2005 to service the new fleet of 3000 Class Railcars, this is located at Fortwilliam, just north of York Road. When another fleet of CAF Railcars (4000 Class) arrived in 2011–12 a new facility was required as there was no scope for expansion at Fortwilliam. The redundant permanent way depot at Adelaide, just south of Belfast, was cleared and a new depot and servicing facility built on its site. This depot maintains and services both classes of CAF Railcar.

▲ The interior of one of the refurbished Irish Rail 22000 Class InterCity Railcars, 5-car set 22039 – the seats have been reupholstered with leather upholstery. Note how almost all of the seats are arranged in bays of four which line up with the windows. **Robert Pritchard**

▼ With the city of Belfast a distant backdrop, 4013 passes through the train wash at Adelaide depot on 13 March 2014. The small permanent way yard can be seen to the left. **Robert Pritchard**

IRISH RAILFREIGHT TODAY

Having experienced some modest growth after an all-time low in 2009, rail freight traffic in Ireland has stabilised in recent years and there have been relatively few changes to report. Ireland is a small country with little manufacturing industry and it has always been difficult to make freight pay. However now Irish Rail has removed the loss-making traffic and concentrated on bulk flows the freight side of the business has been showing a profit. Cement, shale and sugarbeet trains are all now long-gone, but intermodal traffic has been fairly buoyant, despite the loss of the DFDS Ballina–Waterford container trains in June 2018 (IWT has since taken over some of the lost DFDS traffic, which has instead been moved to and from Dublin Port).

In addition to infrastructure trains there are three main flows – containers, timber and zinc ore. Paths are as described at the time of writing. Because of the long single track sections on both the Waterford and Westport/Ballina lines, freights tend to stick to the booked paths, which change little year-on-year.

- **Containers**: Irish logistics company International Warehousing & Transport (IWT) uses rail to move Coca Cola concentrate from Ballina Beverages to Dublin Port for export. The terminal at Ballina is also used as a hub for the north and North West of Ireland, and pharmaceutical and retail products are conveyed to Ballina. From May 2019 IWT increased services by 30%, from 14 to 18 trains a week – nine in each direction. The normal pattern of operation (two trains in one direction and one train in the other direction, alternating each day) is shown in the Table below. Trains can be worked by either 201s or 071s. During the first part of 2020 some trial intermodal services also operated from Ballina to Waterford for XPO Logistics, conveying refrigerated products and returning intermodal trains to Waterford for the first time since the DFDS trains were withdrawn. It was hoped that a regular service could be introduced during the latter part of 2020.

- **Timber**: Timber traffic is carried for the Irish state forestry company Coillte from Ballina and Westport to the pulp mill at Waterford where it is used for the manufacture of building products, most of which are exported. A typical week will see two loaded trains leaving County Mayo and two sets of empties returning north. The destination can be swapped between Westport and Ballina as required. All trains reverse at Kildare and are normally in the hands of 071s. Times are shown in the Table.

- **Zinc ore**: The most intense freight operation is the trains of zinc ore from the Tara mines at Navan (west of Drogheda on the former Navan passenger line) to Dublin Port for export. Navan is Europe's largest zinc mine. From North Wall these trains operate along the tramway type lines in the road to the Port. There are normally two return trips that run on Mondays–Fridays – sometimes a third may run in the evening. Departure times for the loaded trains from Tara Mines are normally 09.20 and 12.20 with returns for the empties from Dublin Port at 14.00 and 18.50. These trains are solidly operated by 071s.

Infrastructure trains tend to be centred on the large permanent way yard at Portlaoise which acts as the central hub for ballast, sleeper and rail trains. Ballast trains can also often be seen at the quarry at Lisduff, between Ballybrophy and Templemore, or the loading point alongside the station at Portarlington. The important wagon repair depot at Limerick also generates some trains.

Apart from infrastructure trains there is no rail freight in Northern Ireland. Infrastructure trains may be seen operating from the permanent way yard at Ballymena, or the smaller yards at Adelaide (Belfast) or Poyntzpass. These duties are covered by NIR's three 111 Class locomotives.

IWT container trains

Mondays
08.15 Ballina–Dublin
09.35 Dublin–Ballina
10.05 Ballina–Dublin
Tuesdays
09.35 Dublin–Ballina
10.05 Ballina–Dublin
13.40 Dublin–Ballina
Wednesdays
08.15 Ballina–Dublin
09.35 Dublin–Ballina
10.05 Ballina–Dublin

Thursdays
09.35 Dublin–Ballina
10.05 Ballina–Dublin
13.40 Dublin–Ballina
Fridays
08.15 Ballina–Dublin
09.35 Dublin–Ballina
10.05 Ballina–Dublin
Saturdays
08.15 Ballina–Dublin
09.35 Dublin–Ballina
13.40 Dublin–Ballina

Coillte Timber trains

Mondays
11.05 Ballina–Waterford
11.30 Waterford–Westport
Thursdays
11.00 Westport–Waterford
11.30 Waterford–Ballina

▲ In CIÉ black and tan livery 071 approaches Killarney Bridge, near Thomastown, County Kilkenny with the 11.05 Westport–Waterford fully-laden timber train on 7 June 2018. **Finbarr O'Neill**

▼ InterCity-liveried 234 is seen crossing the Curragh near Kildare with the 08.15 Ballina–Dublin North Wall container train on 13 September 2019. **Robert Pritchard**

CURRENT OPERATIONS: IRISH RAIL

Despite the loss of most of the loco-hauled trains there is still much to interest the enthusiast in Ireland. Service frequencies and journey times across most routes have been improved enormously and although lacking the character of the loco-hauled trains they replaced, the InterCity Railcars that work most trains are very comfortable to travel on and have been broadly welcomed by Irish Rail staff and passengers alike.

The Irish Rail routes, frequency of service and stock used on each route at the time of writing (based on the full Monday–Friday timetable as operated before the reduced coronavirus timetables were introduced in March 2020) is listed below. Long single track sections on most Irish Rail routes mean that timetables change little year-to-year, aside from when there is a major recast. For more information readers are advised to visit the IR website at www.irishrail.ie where timetables can be downloaded or printed out in pdf form.

The population of Ireland in 2019 was around 6.8 million, the split being around 4.9 million in the Republic and 1.9 million in Northern Ireland. The two capitals are by far the biggest cities in both countries, the population of the Dublin urban area being around 1.3 million whilst Belfast has around 280 000 inhabitants.

Dublin Heuston–Cork: This is Irish Rail's prime route linking its two biggest cities (Cork has a population of around 125 000) and the distance between the them is 165½ miles. There is an hourly service in each direction between 07.00 and 19.00. End-to-end times are now around 2h30, with trains generally calling at around four stations out of Portlaoise, Ballybrophy, Templemore, Thurles, Limerick Junction, Charleville and Mallow depending on the times of connecting trains (all, except one non-stop train, call at Mallow for Tralee and Limerick Junction for Limerick) and also to give a spread of services to the more remote stations. The one non-stop train from Cork to Dublin completes the journey in 2h15. The majority of services are in the hands of loco-hauled Mark 4 sets, hauled by 201s. 22000 Railcars are booked for some trains: normally the 10.00, 12.00 (SX), 14.00 (FX), 19.00 (FO) and 21.00 (FX) from Dublin and 05.50, 06.15, 13.25, 15.25 (SX) and 17.25 (FX) from Cork are InterCity Railcars.

Dublin Heuston–Galway/Westport & Ballina: The line to Galway, the Republic of Ireland's fourth largest city at around 80 000 and 129½ miles from Dublin Heuston, is busy with leisure travellers and has seen a large increase in the number of trains since the introduction of 22000 Railcars. On Mon–Sat there are nine trains a day from Heuston to Galway with an additional peak-hour train to and from Athlone plus an early morning Athlone–Galway and evening Galway–Athlone. Journey time is generally around 2h15 with calls at Portarlington, Tullamore, Clara (not all trains), Athlone, Ballinasloe and Athenry, with most trains also calling at Oranmore and a few at Woodlawn and Attymon.

The longer route to Westport leaves the Galway line just after Athlone and has four through trains a day to Dublin and one extra on Fridays. There are five trains from Westport to Dublin on Mondays–Fridays. The last section of this route is highly scenic as it passes through County Mayo. Westport is 164 miles from Heuston and trains generally take 3h10, calling at Portarlington, Tullamore, Clara, Athlone, Roscommon, Castlerea, Ballyhaunis, Claremorris, Manulla Junction and Castlebar. All trains are worked by 22000s. Manulla Junction is unique in that it is purely an interchange station, with no access possible on or off the platform. Passengers change here for the shuttle to Ballina, which at around 10 000 population is actually larger than neighbouring Westport. A 2-car 2800 Railcar is outbased at Ballina for this duty and the 20½ mile, 28 minute trip is performed seven times a day in both directions to connect with all of the Westport line trains.

Dublin Heuston–Waterford: Waterford is a city of around 53 000 inhabitants and sees seven through trains a day from Dublin (plus one extra on Fridays). The 111-mile route leaves the Dublin–Cork line at Cherryville Junction, just beyond Kildare. All trains are 22000s with a journey time of around 2h10 and a typical stopping pattern of Kildare, Athy, Carlow, Muine Bheag (Bagenalstown), Kilkenny and Thomastown (some trains also call at Hazelhatch, Sallins & Naas and/or Newbridge). A morning semi-fast from Waterford takes 1h53, being booked to use the Kilkenny avoiding line (trains have to reverse when calling at this station). The Friday additional trains also avoid Kilkenny. There are also morning and evening peak trains from Carlow to Dublin and a mid-evening train in the other direction.

Other direct trains from Dublin Heuston: As well as the routes listed above there are also daily direct trains linking Dublin and Tralee (07.05 ex-Tralee and 17.05 ex-Heuston Mon–Sat). At 3h45 for the distance of 206½ miles this is Irish Rail's longest distance train, Tralee also being the most westerly main line station in Europe. On Sundays there are three trains from Tralee to Dublin and two in the opposite direction, reflecting the fact that Killarney is a popular tourist destination (for the national park and County Kerry coastline).

There are relatively few through trains from Dublin to Limerick, Ireland's third city with a population of 94 000. There are trains from Dublin at 15.30, 16.25 and 17.25 and back from Limerick at 05.30, 06.40, 07.40 and 08.55. At other times passengers must use Cork trains and change at Limerick Junction for a shuttle to Limerick. The 05.30, 08.55 and 16.25 run via Limerick Jn whilst the others use the Limerick Jn west avoiding curve.

Heuston commuter services: Most Dublin Heuston commuter trains run to and from Portlaoise. During the day there is a roughly hourly service on this route, with some additional peak-hour trains also running to or from Newbridge, Kildare or Portarlington. In 2016 a new service commenced from Grand Canal Dock and Dublin Connolly to Hazelhatch, bringing passenger services back to the Phoenix Park Tunnel line, which serves the remote Platform 10 at Heuston (although this is used for crew changes only, not as a passenger stop). An hourly services operates from Grand Canal Dock to Hazelhatch, with peak-hour additionals to Newbridge. These trains run on Mondays–Fridays only.

Dublin Connolly–Belfast: The "Enterprise" service between Dublin and Belfast (113½ miles) is operated jointly by IR and NIR. There are eight trains a day in each direction, most calling at Drogheda, Dundalk, Newry and Portadown. Sundays see five trains in each direction. Journeys are timed to take between 2h5 and 2h15. All trains are booked for 201 locomotives with the De Dietrich stock but IR 29000 Class or NIR 3000 Class Railcars can stand-in if required.

Dublin Connolly–Sligo: There are eight return trips from Connolly to Sligo (135 miles from Dublin, population 20 000) with most trains calling at Drumcondra, Maynooth, Kilcock, Enfield, Mullingar, Edgeworthstown, Longford, Dromod, Carrick-on-Shannon, Boyle, Ballymote and Collooney. Most trains are worked by 22000s but there are still some diagrams for 29000 Class sets. There are also two peak-hour trains to and from Longford and one evening train to Mullingar.

Dublin Connolly–Rosslare: Trains that take the route along the east coast of the country to Rosslare start in one of the through platforms at Connolly. There are four trains a day that undertake the 105-mile journey, and a fifth that runs to Wexford only and starts from Gorey on the return. Rosslare itself is very small and best known for the ferry connections to a number of destinations, including Fishguard, but Wexford (population 20 000) is a popular tourist destination. Trains call at Tara Street, Pearse, Dun Laoghaire, Bray, Greystones, Wicklow, Rathdrum, Arklow, Gorey, Enniscorthy, Wexford, Rosslare Strand and Rosslare Europort and some also call at Kilcoole.

DART and Connolly/Docklands commuter services:
The DART service was revamped in September 2018 and a new ten minute service was introduced. Between 07.00 and 20.00 there is a service every ten minutes in each direction between Bray and Howth Junction, with trains then running to either Howth or Malahide. One train in every three starts back from Greystones. In total 32 route miles are electrified that make up the DART system, the 3½ mile branch off the main line to Howth is the only section exclusively served by DART electrics.

Diesel suburban services are dominated by 29000 Railcars, supplemented by some 22000 Railcars outbased at Drogheda. A complex service operates between Drogheda and Dublin Pearse with peak and some off-peak trains extended to and from Dundalk or Bray. In the morning peak there is also a train that starts back from Newry (at 06.30), providing the only local cross-border service. On the western route to Maynooth, in addition to the Sligo trains, a half-hourly service operates during the day between Connolly and Maynooth. There is also an hourly service to M3 Parkway. During the day this operates as a shuttle from Clonsilla, and at peak times at up to half-hourly frequency from Docklands station, which opened in 2007 to serve the growing number of offices around the area and also relieve pressure on Connolly.

Limerick–Ennis–Galway: Ennis (population 25 000) is an important town and the capital of County Clare. A service of nine trains a day link Limerick with Ennis, with five of these continuing to Galway via the Western Rail Corridor, which reopened in 2010. This line joins the Dublin–Galway line at Athenry. Most trains are 2800 Railcars, although some 22000s also work the route.

Limerick–Ballybrophy: This scenic secondary route includes stations at Castleconnell, Birdhill, Nenagh, Cloughjordan and Roscrea, all serving small communities. The line has a longstanding service of just two trains a day in each direction, Mon–Sat, plus a Mon–Fri morning peak train from Nenagh into Limerick. On Sundays there is just one train in the evening in each direction. Journey time for the 57 miles is a rather slow 2h–2h10 as a result of a large number of permanent speed restrictions. Trains are operated by 2800s.

Limerick–Limerick Junction–Waterford: Limerick Junction–Limerick sees a frequent, roughly hourly, service during the day, providing connections to and from Dublin–Cork trains. Some continue to Ennis or Galway via the Western Rail Corridor. This means that Cork–Galway journeys can be completed with just one change. Trains are a mix of 2800s and 22000s. Two trains a day in each direction run between Waterford and Limerick Junction, calling at Carrick-on-Suir, Clonmel, Cahir and Tipperary. These trains are 22000s and take 1h45–1h50 to complete the 56 miles. On departure from Limerick Junction trains head west as if continuing to Limerick and then reverse and cross the Dublin–Cork main line on a flat crossing.

Mallow–Tralee: At 62 miles this is the longest branch line, although it does have a small number of through trains from Dublin, as detailed above. During the day there is a two-hourly shuttle between Mallow and Tralee, worked by 22000s and calling at Banteer, Millstreet, Rathmore, Killarney and Farranfore. These take around 1h35, the station layout at Killarney requiring a double reversal. A number of trains work through to and from Cork.

Cork–Cobh/Midleton: The Cork suburban service comprises hourly trains on the two short branches to Cobh and Midleton, with extras at peak times. All trains are worked by 2600 Railcars, with 4-cars on some peak trains. The 2600s also operate some peak-hour extra trains between Cork and Mallow and some trains to Tralee at weekends.

CURRENT OPERATIONS: NIR

In addition to the Enterprise there are three distinct routes in Northern Ireland, the busy Bangor–Belfast–Portadown route, plus the Belfast–Larne and Belfast–Londonderry/Portrush lines.

Bangor–Belfast–Portadown: This route sees a basic half-hourly service through the day Mon–Sat (hourly on Sundays), supplemented by additional Bangor–Lisburn trains at Mon–Fri peak times, some of these run fast between Bangor West and Holywood and some trains also run fast between Lisburn and Great Victoria Street. Some balancing trains even run non-stop between Bangor and Belfast Lanyon Place. Almost all trains operate via the terminus at Belfast Great Victoria Street, the Enterprise being the main service that uses the GVS avoiding line. It is 12½ miles between Belfast Central and Bangor, halfway along the route is Cultra, a short walk from the station is the Ulster Transport Museum. A sparse local service operates at peak times between Portadown and Newry (in addition to the Enterprise), serving the remote stations at Scarva and Poyntzpass. It is 44 miles from Newry into Belfast Central (direct). Trains are worked by a mix of 3000 and 4000 Railcars with some peak trains formed of 6-car sets.

Belfast–Larne Harbour: During the day an hourly service operates between Great Victoria Street and Larne Harbour, a distance of 26 miles. In addition an hourly service also runs from GVS as far as Whitehead. Additional trains run at peak times, some terminating at Carrickfergus with a few trains running non-stop from Lanyon Place to Carrickfergus. On Sundays each service runs two-hourly. Again, 3000 and 4000 units work all services, with 4000s favoured for this line.

Belfast–Londonderry/Portrush: The longest route in Northern Ireland is that from the capital to Londonderry, the country's second biggest city at around 108 000 and a distance of 94 miles (from Belfast Lanyon Place). A 6-mile branch from Coleraine serves the seaside resort of Portrush. During the day there are hourly departures from Great Victoria Street to Londonderry and a connecting shuttle operates to Portrush. The morning peak sees two direct trains from Portrush to GVS and in the evening two from Lanyon Place to Coleraine. Both 3000 and 4000 Railcars are used on the route, although 3000s are favoured because of their additional toilet. Some peak trains are 6-cars. The normal route from Belfast to the north has been via Bleach Green Junction since 2001, although an alternative route, via Lisburn and Crumlin to Antrim, is kept as a diversionary route and is also used by railtours.

HOW TO GET TO IRELAND

The Republic of Ireland and Northern Ireland can easily be reached by sea or air from mainland Britain. The most popular route by sea is from Holyhead to Dublin: Holyhead has a regular train service which includes through trains from London. Rosslare is useful to reach Wexford but following the closure of the Rosslare–Waterford line in 2010 is no longer linked by rail to Waterford (although there are buses).

The Irish Sea can be crossed by several types of vessel; the modern Superferry or Ship (all weathers) and fast HSS or Sea Lynx catamaran (which can be cancelled if the sea gets rough!). Most and Dublin Swift carry foot passengers as well as vehicular traffic. Times given are correct at the time of writing but most have changed little in recent years, although Irish Ferries have recently added more services onto the Holyhead–Dublin route. Stena Line has now finished operating the seasonal Holyhead–Dun Laoghaire route, with all ferries now concentrated on Dublin. P&O has also dropped its summer Troon–Larne route. For up-to-date information readers should check with the relevant operator.

No ferries to Ireland now operate from Stranraer – all routes having transferred to Stena's new port at Cairnryan, which is around four miles from Stranraer and connected by buses, although it is quicker if travelling by train to change at Ayr and catch the direct Stena-operated bus link from there. In Dublin (and Belfast) connecting buses run from the Ports to the city centre, whilst Rosslare is adjacent to Rosslare Europort station.

SEA CROSSINGS

Irish Ferries: www.irishferries.com.

Ship Holyhead–Dublin Ferryport (3h15–3h30). From Holyhead at 02.40, 08.15, 14.10 and 20.15* and from Dublin at 02.00*, 08.05, 14.30 and 20.55 (* no foot passengers allowed).

Fast Ferry Holyhead–Dublin Ferryport (2h15). From Holyhead at 10.40 and 16.45 and from Dublin at 07.30 and 13.50.

Ship Pembroke Dock–Rosslare (4h). From Pembroke at 02.45 and 14.45 and from Rosslare at 08.45 and 20.45.

Stena Line: www.stenaline.co.uk

Superferry Holyhead–Dublin Ferryport (3h15–3h40). From Holyhead at 02.30, 08.55, 14.00 and 20.30 and from Dublin at 02.15, 08.10, 14.50 and 20.40.

Superferry Fishguard–Rosslare (3h15–4h15). From Fishguard at 13.10 and 23.45 and from Rosslare at 08.00 and 18.10.

Superferry Cairnryan–Belfast (2h15–2h20). From Cairnryan and Belfast at 04.00, 09.30, 15.00, 19.30 and 23.30.

Ship Liverpool–Belfast (8h). From Liverpool and Belfast at 10.30 (not on Sundays and Mondays) and 22.30.

P&O Ferries: www.poferries.com

Superferry Cairnryan–Larne (2h). Five crossings Mon–Fri and three per day at weekends.

Ship Liverpool–Dublin (8h–8h30). From Liverpool and Dublin at 09.30 (no foot passengers allowed).

It is also possible to travel by ferry from Cherbourg in Northern France (Irish Ferries) to Dublin and from the Isle of Man to Dublin and Belfast (Isle of Man Steam Packet).

RAIL/SEA

Combined "SailRail" rail and sea tickets are available to foot passengers using Irish Ferries and Stena Line routes. SailRail is a partnership between UK train operating companies, the ferry companies, Irish Rail and Northern Ireland Railways. Fares are based on a zonal system depending on the originating station in Britain. All tickets are Standard Class and offer excellent value for money.

As well as Dublin (it is best to use "Dublin Ferryport" when looking up tickets online), SailRail tickets can also be purchased to all the major Irish Rail and Northern Ireland Railways stations, and Advance fares are available. For example London–Cork via Holyhead is available for as little as £68 and London–Belfast for £61 in 2020. London–Dublin tickets are available from £50 and Birmingham–Dublin for £45.50. The cost of transferring between the port and the city centre (ie in Dublin) is not included.

How to buy combined rail/sea tickets

- In person at staffed British railway stations.
- By calling the SailRail booking line on 08709 000 773. Lines are open 08.00–20.00 Mondays–Saturdays and 09.00–17.00 on Sundays.
- SailRail tickets can be purchased online via any train operators website, and can then be picked up from "Fast-ticket" machine at stations.

AIR

It is possible to fly from most of the airports in mainland Britain to the Republic of Ireland and Northern Ireland. The airline fare structure is complex. Usually the earlier you book, the cheaper fare you can obtain. There are also many flights from Continental Europe. Readers are recommended to consult a flight comparison website such as www.skyscanner.net or check individual operators websites (two of the major players are Aer Lingus and Ryanair).

NORTHERN IRELAND

It is possible to fly direct into three airports in the province – Belfast International, Belfast City and Londonderry.

REPUBLIC OF IRELAND

Most visitors are likely to arrive into the major airport at Dublin, but there are also other airports at Cork, Donegal, Kerry, Ireland West (Knock), Shannon, and Waterford (the last is currently without passenger services).

IRISH ROVER TICKETS

A range of Rover tickets are available to enjoy unlimited travel on the Railways of Ireland. Unfortunately, the "Emerald Card" offering travel in both the Republic and Northern Ireland was withdrawn in 2009 and the only alternative is the rather more expensive InterRail Ireland pass. The Irish Explorer rail and bus 8 day ticket has also more recently been withdrawn. There is no rover ticket that covers Northern Ireland on its own apart from the NIR Sunday day ticket. However, you can purchase an "iLINK" smartcard and for £16.50 load on to it a day's unlimited travel. This works out cheaper than a day return from Belfast to Londonderry. Meanwhile, the "DART Rambler" ticket or "Leap" smartcard offer good value for exploring the Dublin area, including the highly scenic section of the DART to Greystones.

Full details are shown in the listing below with prices applicable at the time of going to press. Adult prices are shown, Child prices tend to be roughly half the adult price. Irish Rail and Luas tickets are shown in Euros (€), with conversion to pounds at the conversion rate at the time of writing (€1 = approximately 91p).

None of the tickets listed have any time restrictions.

InterRail One Country Ireland pass: Valid for a period of 3, 4, 5, 6 or 8 days in one month. Pass must be purchased in advance, this can be done via the website www.interrail.eu. The InterRail pass also gives a 30% discount on foot crossings to Ireland by ferry with Irish Ferries and Stena Line. "Youth" prices for those aged 25 or under are 35% cheaper than the full adult prices (Standard Class only). Children aged 4–11 can travel for half the adult price.

3 days in one month: Standard Class £109, First Class £145.
4 days in one month: Standard Class £131, First Class £175.
5 days in one month: Standard Class £152, First Class £203.
6 days in one month: Standard Class £171, First Class £228.
8 days in one month: Standard Class £206, First Class £275.

IR "Irish Explorer" (rail only): 5 days out of 15 for unlimited travel on all Irish Rail services, but not on the cross-border Enterprise service north of Dundalk: €160 (around £145.50).

IR "Trekker Four Day" (rail only): 4 consecutive days travel on all Irish Rail services, but not on the Enterprise north of Dundalk: €110 (around £100).

IR "DART Rambler": Unlimited travel on inner Dublin area suburban services (not just on the DART electric services), bounded by the following stations – Howth, Balbriggan, M3 Parkway, Kilcock, Sallins & Naas and Kilcoole: Adult 1 day: €12.15 (around £11.05). Family 1 day: €20 (around £18.20). Adult 3 days: €28.50 (around £25.90).

NIR "Sunday Day Tracker": Valid for travel on all NIR services on Sundays: £8.

NIR "iLINK": iLINK is a smartcard that can be purchased free online or for a deposit of £1.50 at stations. Once you have one you can use it as a Rover by paying for unlimited travel (on trains or buses) on a particular day for a number of zones. The zone 1 fare has actually been reduced in price slightly since the last edition of this book, and represents excellent value for the area around Belfast. The 2020 prices are: Zone 1 (Belfast city zone): £5, Zone 2 (Belfast and as far out as Bangor, Lisburn and Antrim): £10, Zone 3 (Belfast and as far out as Larne, Ballymena and Portadown): £13.50, Zone 4 (the whole of Northern Ireland): £16.50. Weekly iLINK fares are also available. For more details and maps see the Translink website.

"Luas Flexi": Unlimited travel on the Luas Red and Green tram lines. 1 day: €7.30 (around £6.60). 7 days: €28 (around £25.45).

The Dublin "Leap" smartcard is also worth considering for regular trips. For tourists there is a "Leap Visitor Card" available for €10 for one day, €19.50 for three days and €40 for seven days. This can be bought in advance from the Leap Card website and also at various outlets, including at the Airport information desk. It is valid on the Airlink 747 and 757 buses to and from the Airport, all Dublin Bus and Go Ahead buses, Luas services and train services in the short-hop zone (the same boundaries as the DART Rambler). See www.dublinpublictransport.ie

ABBREVIATIONS & CODES

Vehicle type codes used in this book generally follow the British system as follows:

B Brake	R Catering vehicle	S Standard (formerly second)
D Driving vehicle	C Composite	O Open
M Motor vehicle (for multiple units)	F First	K Side corridor with toilet

Railway Companies

The following railway company abbreviations are used:

BR	British Railways	LMS	London Midland & Scottish Railway
B&CDR	Belfast & County Down Railway	MGWR	Midland Great Western Railway
CDRJC	County Donegal Railways Joint	NCC	Northern Counties Committee of the
	Committee		Midland Railway (later of the LMS and
CIÉ	Coras Iompair Éireann		British Transport Commission)
C&LR	Cavan & Leitrim Railway	NIR	Northern Ireland Railways
DSER	Dublin & South Eastern Railway	SL&NCR	Sligo Leitrim & Northern Counties
GNR(I)	Great Northern Railway (Ireland)		Railway
GSR	Great Southern Railways	T&DR	Tralee & Dingle Railway
GSWR	Great Southern & Western Railway	UTA	Ulster Transport Authority
IR	Irish Rail (Iarnród Éireann)	WCR	West Clare Railway

Accommodation

Under this heading will be found the number of First Class seats, Standard Class seats and toilets. Accommodation is shown as First Class/Standard Class seats (for example 32/32 means 32 First and 32 Standard Class seats). A figure in brackets (ie (+5)) indicates tip-up seats (in addition to the fixed seats).

Standard Abbreviations Used in Listings

(O)	Outside cylinders on a steam locomotive (the norm is inside cylinders)
(S)	Stored
(3)	3 cylinders on a steam locomotive (the norm is 2)
LC	Level Crossing
Jn	Junction
p	Push-pull fitted
Railcar	Diesel Multiple Unit (the term DMU is not used widely in Ireland).

The EVN numbering system

Irish Rail has been applying 12-digit European Vehicle Numbering (EVN) numbers to its rolling stock in recent years, with stock often given the full number when it is repainted. For some locomotives digits 5–11 of the EVN are carried on the cab front. The IR stock number is usually highlighted in bold as part of the EVN, however, and vehicles are still referred to by their traditional Irish Rail 3, 4 or 5 digit numbers in this publication. European Union and consequently Irish legislation requires "Any vehicle placed in service in the Community rail system shall carry a European Vehicle Number assigned when the first authorisation for placing in service is granted". Northern Ireland Railways stock does not carry EVNs.

The first digit of the EVN is the code for a traction unit with the second giving the type of traction, thus:

90	Steam locomotives
91	Electric locomotives faster than 99 km/h
92	Diesel locomotive faster than 99 km/h
93	High Speed EMU
94	EMU
95	DMU
96	Loose trailers
97	Electric shunting locomotives
98	Diesel shunting locomotives
99	Departmental self-powered vehicles

The second pair of numbers denotes the country code, 60 being Ireland.

▲ An illustration of how the 12-digit EVN is displayed on the side of unit 2817. **Robert Pritchard**

BUILDERS

The following codes are used for builders:

A&O	Alldays & Onions, Birmingham
AtW	Atkinson Walker Wagons Ltd, Preston, Lancashire
BP	Beyer Peacock & Co Ltd, Gorton, Manchester
BRCW	Birmingham Railway Carriage & Wagon Co Ltd, Smethwick, Staffordshire
BREL	British Rail Engineering Ltd, Derby Carriage Works
Brush	Brush Electrical Co Ltd, Loughborough, Leicestershire
Bury	Bury, Curtis & Kennedy, Liverpool
CIÉ	Córas Iompair Éireann, Inchicore Works, Dublin
Crewe	London & North Western Railway, Crewe Works
DC	Drewry Car Co Ltd, London (suppliers only)
DDF	De Dietrich, Reichshoffen, France
Derby	London, Midland & Scottish Railway, Derby Works
Deutz	Motorenfabrik Deutz AG, Cologne, Germany
Doncaster	British Rail, Doncaster Works
Dübs	Dübs & Co Ltd, Glasgow
EEV	English Electric Co Ltd, Vulcan Works, Newton-le-Willows, Lancashire
GM	General Motors, La Grange, Illinois, USA
GNR(I)	Great Northern Railway, Dundalk Works
GSWR	Great Southern & Western Railway, Inchicore Works, Dublin
GSR	Great Southern Railway, Inchicore Works, Dublin
HE	Hunslet Engine Co Ltd, Leeds
LHB	Linke Hofmann Busch, Salzgitter, Germany
K	Kitson & Co Ltd, Leeds
MaK	Maschinenbau Kiel GmBH, Kiel, Germany
Milnes	GF Milnes & Co Ltd, Hadley, Shropshire
MV	Metropolitan-Vickers Electrical Co Ltd, Trafford Park, Manchester (locos listed erected at Dunkinfield Carriage Works)
NBL	North British Locomotive Co Ltd, Glasgow
NCC	Northern Counties Committee, York Road Works, Belfast
NR	Neilson Reid & Co Ltd, Glasgow
NW	Nasmyth Wilson & Co Ltd, Patricoft, Lancashire
PRV	Park Royal Vehicles Ltd, Park Royal, London
RS	Robert Stephenson & Co Ltd, Newcastle-upon-Tyne
SS	Sharp Stewart & Co Ltd, Manchester
WkB	Walker Bros (Wigan) Ltd, Wigan, Lancashire.

LINKS TO USEFUL WEBSITES

Links to museum and heritage line websites are given in the Museums section.

Irish Rail: www.irishrail.ie
Northern Ireland Railways: www.translink.co.uk
Luas Light Rail system: www.luas.ie
Transport Infrastructure Ireland: www.tii.ie
Irish Railway Record Society: www.irrs.ie
Irish Traction Group: www.irishtractiongroup.com
Railway Preservation Society of Ireland: www.steamtrainsireland.com
Tourist information: www.discoverireland.com

1. IRISH RAIL ROLLING STOCK

LIVERIES

In the 1990s and early 2000s Irish Rail locomotives and loco-hauled coaches were traditionally painted in orange & black livery. From 2005 a new silver and green livery was introduced on the 201 locomotives that matched the then newly delivered Mark 4 rolling stock. Most of the 071s received a black and silver freight livery when they were refurbished in 2008–09 but this was superseded in 2013 by a new "slate grey" colour scheme that is now carried by all 071s apart from two which have been specially repainted back into the "retro" liveries as special heritage repaints.

The older diesel Railcars were initially given the orange & black livery before being painted into a predominantly lime green Commuter livery in the 2000s. This was superseded by a silver & green livery, initially reserved for the 22000 InterCity Railcars but later also applied to the older Railcars. The 29000 Class suburban railcars have been receiving a different two-tone mainly dark green livery since 2014.

DART EMUs have always been painted in the special two-tone green "DART" livery with a yellow stripe.

The following livery codes are used in this book:

BE Belmond Pullman (dark blue).
BT Black and tan livery (orange with a broad black stripe).
C "Commuter" Railcar livery (blue lower bodyside, lime green upper bodyside separated by a broad white stripe. Yellow ends surrounded by blue. White doors).
E Enterprise (unbranded/common-user livery). Silver & dark grey.
EN Enterprise (new). Silver with a broad black stripe around the windows and broad deep pink and red swooshes on locomotives (deep pink and red stripes on coaching stock).
G New Commuter livery. Mid-green with dark green band around the windows.
GY Slate grey freight livery.
I InterCity (green & silver).
IE Original Iarnród Éireann livery (orange with a broad black stripe lined out in white).
IS InterCity Railcar (silver with a dark green roof and bodyside stripes).
R Revised orange & black (201 Class) – full yellow ends.

▲ New Enterprise-liveried 8209 arrives at Belfast Lanyon Place with the 15.20 from Dublin Connolly on 14 September 2019. To the left stands 216 with the Belmond Grand Hibernian. **Robert Pritchard**

1.1. DIESEL LOCOMOTIVES

071 CLASS   Co-Co

Once top-link passenger locos, these locos are now used on freight and infrastructure duties across the Irish Rail network, along with occasional railtours and special trains. A major overhaul programme took place between 2013 and 2018 which saw every loco rebuilt, including an engine rebuild, refurbished bogies and cabs and a new grey livery (except 071 and 073 repainted into the retro 1976 and 1987 style orange livery).

Built: 1976 by General Motors, La Grange, Illinois, USA. 18 built.
Engine: General Motors 12-cylinder 645 E3C developing of 1830 kW (2450 hp) gross at 900 rpm with 1675 kW (2250 hp) available for traction.
Transmission: Electric. 6 axle-hung nose-suspended General Motors D77B traction motors.
Maximum Tractive Effort: 289 kN (65 000 lbf).
Continuous Tractive Effort: 192 kN (43 160 lbf) at 15.1 mph.
Power At Rail: 1360 kW (1825 hp).
Weight: 99 tonnes.   **Length Over Buffers:** 17.37 m.
Wheel Diameter: 1016 mm.   **Train Brakes:** Air and Vacuum.
Multiple Working: With GM locos.   **Maximum Speed:** 90 mph.
Home depot: Inchicore.

071	BT	076	GY	081	GY	085	GY
072	GY	077	GY	082	GY	086	GY
073	IE	078	GY	083	GY	087	GY
074	GY	079	GY	084	GY	088	GY
075	GY	080	GY				

Name: 082 CUMANN NA nINNEALTÓIRÍ – THE INSTITUTION OF ENGINEERS OF IRELAND

▲ Repainted into its original 1976 "black and tan" livery, pioneer 071 passes Dunkitt on the approach to Waterford with the RPSI's "071 40th Anniversary" tour from Dublin to Waterford on 13 May 2016.   **Finbarr O'Neill**

▲ In the standard "slate grey" livery, 079 hauls a train of eight ballast hoppers through Nenagh on a glorious 15 April 2020 while working from Ballybrophy to Limerick, after it had dropped ballast near Borris-in-Ossory.
Neil Dinnen

201 CLASS
Co-Co

Once the flagship of the locomotive fleet, 11 of these locos (mainly those without push-pull equipment) are in long-term store following the reduction in the number of loco-hauled services in the late 2000s. Of the remaining locos, around 20 are kept in an active pool to cover the Dublin–Cork passenger service (six locos normally in traffic plus one spare at Cork and one at Inchicore) and Dublin–Belfast Enterprise (three in traffic plus one spare at Dublin Connolly and one at Belfast York Road). The remaining locos are used on freight, principally the IWT container trains, or the Belmond "Grand Hibernian" train, to which Belmond-liveried 216 is normally dedicated. 230 is stored following fire damage sustained in 2013. 225 returned to service in October 2019 after some nine years out of traffic, but 224 was taken out of traffic in July 2020 after a crack in the underframe was discovered.

Built: 1994–95 by General Motors, London, Ontario, Canada. 34 built.
Engine: General Motors 12 cylinder 710G3B developing 2385 kW (3200 hp) at 900 rpm.
Transmission: Electric. 6 axle-hung nose-suspended General Motors D43 traction motors.

Maximum Tractive Effort:	**Continuous Tractive Effort:** 242 kN (54 400 lbf).
Power At Rail: 1710 kW (2295 hp).	**Weight:** 112 tonnes.
Length Over Buffers: 20.95 m.	**Wheel Diameter:** 1016 mm.
Train Brakes: Air and Vacuum.	**Multiple Working:** With GM locos.
Train Heating: 380 V AC three-phase.	**Maximum Speed:** 100 mph.
Home depot: Inchicore.	

n   Owned by Translink Northern Ireland Railways.
p   Push-pull fitted.
*   TPWS fitted for use on the Belfast–Dublin Enterprise (can also be used on other services).
(S) Stored at Inchicore Works.
[1]   Nameplate carried on one side only.

			English name	Irish name
201 (S)	R		RIVER SHANNON	
202 (S)	R		RIVER LEE	ABHAINN NA LAOI
203 (S)	R		RIVER CORRIB	ABHAINN NA COIRIBE
204 (S)	R		RIVER BARROW	ABHAINN NA BEARÚ
205 (S)	R		RIVER NORE	ABHAINN NA FEÓIRE
206	EN	p*		
207	EN	p*	RIVER BOYNE	ABHAINN NA BÓINNE
8208	EN	pn*		
8209	EN	pn*		
210 (S)	R		RIVER ERNE	ABHAINN NA HÉIRNE
211 (S)	R			
212 (S)	R		RIVER SLANEY	ABHAINN NA SLAINE
213 (S)	R		RIVER MOY	ABHAINN NA MUAIDHE
214 (S)	R		RIVER BROSNA	ABHAINN NA BROSANÍ
215	I	p	RIVER AVONMORE	AN ABHAINN MHÓR[1]
216	BE	p	RIVER DODDER	ABHAINN NA DOTHRA
217	I	p	RIVER FLESK	ABHAINN NA FLEÍSCE
218	I	p	RIVER GARAVOGUE	
219	I	p	RIVER TOLKA	
220	I	p	RIVER BLACKWATER	AN ABHAINN DHUBH
221	I	p	RIVER FEALGE	ABHAINN NA FÉILGE
222	I	p	RIVER DARGLE	
223	I	p	RIVER ANNER	ABHAINN NA HAINNIRE
224 (S)	I	p		ABHAINN NA FÉILE
225	I	p	RIVER DEEL	ABHAINN NA DAOILE
226	I	p		ABHAINN NA SIÚIRE
227	EN	p*	RIVER LAUNE	
228	EN	p*		AN ABHAINN BHUÍ
229	I	p	RIVER MAINE	ABHAINN NA MAINGE
230 (S)	E	p		
231	E	p*		ABHAINN NA MÁIGHE
232	I	p	RIVER CUMMERAGH	
233	E	p*	RIVER CLARE	ABHAINN NA CHLÁIR
234	I	p		

All locos had both English and Irish names allocated but some were never fitted and some have more recently been removed.
226 also carries a plaque reading "Thurles Station Celebrating 150 Years 1848–1998".

▲ InterCity-liveried 221 passes Cloone, near Templemore, with the 15.00 Dublin Heuston–Cork on 8 June 2020. The was the date that services were ramped up on a number of routes following the emergency Covid-19 timetable, which had seen all loco-hauled sets stood down temporarily: this was the first time that Mark 4 sets had been seen in service for 61 days. **Neil Dinnen**

▶ With their Irish language "River" nameplates visible, 217 and 220 await their next turns at Dublin Heuston station on 10 September 2019. **Robert Pritchard**

▲ Enterprise 201s are sometimes seen on the Cork main line. In a now unbranded common-user livery, 231 passes Kilmallock, between Limerick Junction and Charleville, working the 12.00 Dublin Heuston–Cork on 22 April 2019.　　　　　　　　　　　　　　　　　　　　　　**Finbarr O'Neill**

1.1.2. DIESEL LOCOMOTIVES AWAITING DISPOSAL

141 CLASS　　　　　　　　　　　　　　　　　　　　　　　　　　　　　**Bo-Bo**

Whilst a number have been preserved, five Class 141 "small GMs" are still stored at Inchicore awaiting disposal, having been removed from traffic by Irish Rail in early 2010 (other locomotives have been purchased for preservation – see Preserved Locomotives section). These are basically a double-cab version of the 121 Class.

Built: 1962 by General Motors, La Grange, Illinois, USA. 37 built.
Engine: General Motors 8-cylinder 567C or 645E, twin bank, blower-scavenged, developing 710 kW (950 hp) at 835 rpm.
Transmission: Electric. 4 axle-hung nose-suspended General Motors D57 traction motors.
Maximum Tractive Effort: 156 kN (35 000 lbf).
Continuous Tractive Effort: 135 kN (30 400 lbf) at 8 mph.
Power At Rail: 530 kW (710 hp).
Weight: 67 tonnes.
Length Over Buffers: 13.42 m.
Wheel Diameter: 1016 mm.
Train Brakes: Air and Vacuum.
Multiple Working: With Classes 071/121/141/181/201.
Maximum Speed: 75 mph.

All locomotives listed are stored at Inchicore Works. All are in orange & black livery.

144 (S)	162 (S)	171 (S)	177 (S)
147 (S)			

1.2. IR COACHING STOCK

MARK 4 STOCK

The CAF Mark 4 stock is used between Dublin Heuston and Cork in push-pull formations with 201 Class locomotives. There are enough coaches to make up eight sets, with six sets normally diagrammed daily. The sets do not operate in fixed formations.

Formations are normally 8-cars as Loco + 5 Open Standard + Buffet + Open First + Driving Brake. The locomotives are positioned at the Cork end of the rakes.

DRIVING BRAKE GENERATOR VAN

Built: 2004–05 by CAF, Beasain, Spain.
Accommodation: no seats.
Brakes: Air.
Length: 23.81 m.
Weight: 44.8 tonnes.
Couplers: Scharfenberg (inner end only).

Heating System: Air Conditioning.
Bogies: CAF M88.
Width: 2.85 m.
Maximum Speed: 100 mph.

4001	I	4003	I	4005	I	4007	I
4002	I	4004	I	4006	I	4008	I

OPEN STANDARD

Built: 2004–05 by CAF, Beasain, Spain.
Accommodation: –/69 1TD 1W (2+2 mainly facing).
Heating System: Air Conditioning.
Brakes: Air.
Length: 23.66 m (* 23.81 m).
Weight: 40.6 tonnes (* 41.2 tonnes).
Couplers: Scharfenberg (* end coaches: drop-head Buckeye at outer end).

Bogies: CAF M88.
Width: 2.85 m.
Maximum Speed: 100 mph.

4101	I		4112	I		4123	I		4134	I	
4102	I		4113	I		4124	I		4135	I	*
4103	I		4114	I		4125	I	*	4136	I	
4104	I		4115	I	*	4126	I		4137	I	
4105	I	*	4116	I		4127	I		4138	I	
4106	I		4117	I		4128	I		4139	I	
4107	I		4118	I		4129	I		4140	I	*
4108	I		4119	I		4130	I	*	4141	I	
4109	I		4120	I	*	4131	I		4142	I	
4110	I	*	4121	I		4132	I		4143	I	
4111	I		4122	I		4133	I				

OPEN FIRST

Built: 2004–05 by CAF, Beasain, Spain.
Accommodation: 44/– 1TD 1W (2+1 facing).
Brakes: Air.
Length: 23.66 m.
Weight: 39.6 tonnes.
Couplers: Scharfenberg.

Heating System: Air Conditioning.
Bogies: CAF M88.
Width: 2.85 m.
Maximum Speed: 100 mph.

4201	I	4203	I	4205	I	4207	I
4202	I	4204	I	4206	I	4208	I

▲ Mark 4 Driving Brake Generator Van 4002 leads the 07.00 Cork–Dublin Heuston across the Curragh, near Kildare, on 13 September 2019. The train was being propelled by 226. **Robert Pritchard**

▼ Mark 4 Open First 4206 is seen near Kildare on 13 September 2019. **Robert Pritchard**

RESTAURANT BUFFET STANDARD

Built: 2004–05 by CAF, Beasain, Spain.
Accommodation: –/28 (2+2 mainly facing).
Brakes: Air.
Length: 23.66 m.
Weight: 42.7 tonnes.
Couplers: Scharfenberg.

Heating System: Air Conditioning.
Bogies: CAF M88.
Width: 2.85 m.
Maximum Speed: 100 mph.

| 4401 | I | 4403 | I | 4405 | I | 4407 | I |
| 4402 | I | 4404 | I | 4406 | I | 4408 | I |

DEPARTMENTAL COACH

Former Generating Steam & Brake Van originally converted for use as a weed spray vehicle but now used in the formation of the Sperry ultrasonic test train. It is due to be replaced by the new Track Recording Vehicle, 701. For technical details of original build see page 89.

3187

1.2.2 IR COACHING STOCK AWAITING DISPOSAL

The following Mark 3 coaches are stored out of use

Mark 3 coaches

7161   Inchicore Works (stored for RPSI)
7403   Inchicore Works (retained for possible future departmental use)
7607   Inchicore Works (retained for possible future departmental use)

▲ Former Generating Steam Van 3187 is seen in the formation of the 08.25 Limerick–Ballybrophy Sperry ultrasonic test train at Roscrea on 21 February 2020.   **Neil Dinnen**

1.3. IR DIESEL RAILCARS

2600 CLASS   "ARROW"   2-CAR UNITS

These units are used on Cork area local services, on the Cobh and Midleton branches and also between Cork and Mallow. There are booked duties between Mallow and Tralee at weekends. End gangways are fitted.

Built: 1993 by Tokyu Car Corporation, Yokohama, Japan.
Formation: DMSO(A)–DMSO(B).
Wheel Arrangement: B-2 + 2-B.
Accommodation: –/58 1TD 1W + –/71 (2+2 facing).
Weight: 41.2 + 40.2 tonnes.
Engine: One Cummins NTA-855-R1 of 260 kW (350 hp) per car.
Generator: Cummins 6B5.9 GR nishion generator.
Transmission: Hydraulic. A Niigatta DW14G transmission, featuring hydraulic torque converter, is coupled directly to the engine from where the drive is taken through two direct drive geared stages and a forward/reverse gear group to Goko Seisakusho reduction gearboxes on each of the driven axles.
Bogies: Tokyu.   **Length Over Couplers:** 20.26 + 20.26 m.
Width: 2.90 m.   **Wheel Diameter:** 840 mm.
Brakes: Air.   **Maximum Speed:** 70 mph.
Couplers: Dellner automatic (between units), bar (within unit).
Home depot: Limerick (for major maintenance, stabling and fuelling takes place at Cork).

2609 was a maintenance spare vehicle which was stripped for spares, however in 2006 it was refurbished and paired with 2716 to create a 2600 Class/2700 Class hybrid unit. In 2012 the unit was stored at Cork.

2601	2602	**IS**	2607	2608	**IS**	2613	2610	**IS**	2617	2614	**IS**
2603	2604	**IS**	2611	2612	**IS**	2615	2606	**IS**	2609	2716	**C** (S)
2605	2616	**IS**									

2700 CLASS   "ARROW"   2-CAR UNITS

Following a review of the Irish Rail fleet in 2012 these units were stored and their duties in the Limerick area transferred to 2800 Class sets. All units had received overhauls which saw the end gangways sealed up. These units are fitted with a different kind of seating to the 2600s, arranged mostly unidirectionally.

Various proposals have been examined over the years to return these units to traffic, but a tender issued to completely overhaul and refurbish the units in 2018 only returned one compliant and overpriced bid (in the region of €33 million) so for now they remain in long-term storage.

Built: 1997–98 by Alstom, Spain. Nicknamed "Sparrows" (Spanish Arrows).
Formation: DMSO(A)–DMSO(B).
Wheel Arrangement: B-2 + 2-B.
Accommodation: –/50 (+1) 1TD 1W + –/62 (2+2 mainly unidirectional).
Weight: 42.2 + 41.5 tonnes.
Engine: One Cummins NTA-855-R1 of 260 kW (350 hp) per car.
Transmission: Hydraulic. Niigatta DW14G.
Bogies: Alstom.
Length Over Couplers: 20.55 + 20.55 m.
Width: 2.83 m.
Wheel Diameter: 840 mm.
Brakes: Air.
Couplers: Dellner automatic (between units), bar (within unit).
Maximum Speed: 75 mph.
Home depot: All units stored.
Storage locations: Inchicore Works: 2701/02, 2703/04, 2705/06, 2707/08, 2711/12, 2715/24, 2721/20, 2723/26.
                       Cork: 2709/10, 2713/14, 2717/18, 2719/22.

2701	2702	**IS** (S)	2707	2708	**C** (S)	2713	2714	**C** (S)	2719	2722	**IS** (S)
2703	2704	**IS** (S)	2709	2710	**C** (S)	2715	2724	**C** (S)	2721	2720	**C** (S)
2705	2706	**C** (S)	2711	2712	**C** (S)	2717	2718	**IS** (S)	2723	2726	**IS** (S)

▲ 4-car 2600 Class formations are used on some peak-hour services from Cork. On the glorious evening of 13 September 2019 2603/04+2601/02 arrive at Carrigaloe operating the 17.30 Cork–Cobh.
Robert Pritchard

▲ 2800 Class 2809/10 leaves Limerick with the 16.50 shuttle to Limerick Junction on 12 September 2019. **Robert Pritchard**

▼ 2814/13 pass Clareabbey, just south of Ennis, County Clare, with the 13.25 Ennis–Limerick on 13 January 2018. **Neil Dinnen**

2750 CLASS   "ARROW"   SINGLE-CAR UNITS

In 2012 these units were stored, along with the 2700 Class. Both had been overhauled and had their end gangways sealed up.

Built: 1998 by Alstom, Spain. Nicknamed "Sparrows" (Spanish Arrows).
Formation: DMSO.
Wheel Arrangement: B-2.
Accommodation: –/50 (+3) 1TD 1W (2+2 mainly unidirectional).
Weight: 44.8 tonnes.
Engine: One Cummins NTA-855-R1 of 260 kW (350 hp).
Transmission: Hydraulic. Niigata DW14G.
Bogies: Alstom.
Length Over Couplers: 21.592 m.
Width: 2.83 m.
Wheel Diameter: 840 mm.
Brakes: Air.
Couplers: Dellner automatic.
Maximum Speed: 75 mph.
Home depot: N/A.
Storage locations: Cork: 2751.
                   Inchicore Works: 2753.

2751	IS (S)		2753	IS (S)

2800 CLASS   "ARROW"   2-CAR UNITS

Originally these units were used on the Dublin Connolly commuter routes and also on the Rosslare line. Now they are based at Limerick and used on Limerick–Limerick Junction, Limerick–Ennis–Galway (Western Rail Corridor) and Limerick–Ballybrophy via Nenagh. One set is outbased at Ballina for use on the Ballina–Manulla Junction shuttle (there is a booked weekly swap between Limerick and Ballina via Galway to exchange this set). All units have been refurbished with end gangways sealed up.

Built: 2000 by Tokyu Car Corporation, Yokohama, Japan. Fitted with Richmond seating.
Formation: DMSO(A)–DMSO(B).
Wheel Arrangement: B-2 + 2-B.
Accommodation: –/39 1TD 1W + –/46 (2+2 mainly unidirectional).
Weight: 43.9 + 42.6 tonnes.
Engine: One Cummins NTA-855-R1 of 260 kW (350 hp) per car.
Transmission: Hydraulic.
Bogies: Mitsui.
Length Over Couplers: 20.73 + 20.73 m.
Width: 2.90 m.
Wheel Diameter: 840 mm.
Brakes: Air.
Couplers: Dellner automatic (between units), bar (within unit).
Maximum Speed: 75 mph.
Home depot: Limerick.

2801	2802	IS		2807	2808	IS		2813	2814	IS		2817		2818	IS
2803	2804	IS		2809	2810	IS		2815	2816	IS		2819		2820	IS
2805	2806	IS		2811	2812	IS									

22000 CLASS   3-CAR, 4-CAR & 5-CAR INTER-CITY UNITS

The 63 22000s are Irish Rail's InterCity Railcars which entered traffic between 2007 and 2012. They operate across the whole country on InterCity, outer suburban, commuter and also on some regional services such as Waterford–Limerick Junction.

There have been five separate orders for 22000 Class vehicles. The original order in December 2004 was for 120 vehicles, and this was increased in December 2005 to 150 vehicles (formed as 30 3-car sets and ten 6-car sets with First Class and buffets). In March 2007 the order was increased for a third time to 183 vehicles – the additional 33 vehicles being for outer suburban use to replace the Mark 3 push-pull sets (five extra Standard Class only 6-car sets and one further 3-car set). Finally, in December 2008 there was a fourth order for another 51 vehicles, to be formed as 17 3-car sets for use on outer suburban work. This took the total number of vehicles to 234, formed as 48 3-cars (22001–030/046–063) and 15 6-cars (22031–045). In 2019 a further 41 vehicles were ordered (see below).

In 2013–14 more than half the fleet was reformed to give some 4- and 5-car units to better match demand on many routes and also give the flexibility to operate 3-, 4-, 6-, 7- or 8-car formations. The reforming programme was quite complex and involved the following:

22001–010 remained as 3-cars;
22011–030 were increased from 3- to 4-cars with the addition of vehicles from sets 22031–045;
22031–040 (the sets with First Class) were reduced from 6- to 5-cars;
22041–045 were reduced from 6- to 4-cars;
22046–063 remained as 3-cars.

The vehicles that transferred between units 22031–045 to 22011–030 were also renumbered, although some also still carry their original number!

Original-build 3-car units 22010 and 22011 were badly damaged during shipment in summer 2007 after being stored next to fertiliser. They were returned to Korea for rebuilding (the original bodyshells were reused but the electrics renewed) and returned to Ireland with the final batch of units.

In October 2019 41 additional ICR vehicles were ordered. These will be delivered from late 2021. During 2022 it is planned that the fleet formations will be changed again, to create some 6-car sets. The current

▲ 4-car 22000 Class 22020 arrives into Arklow with the 09.33 Dublin Connolly–Rosslare Europort on 10 March 2019.   **Finbarr O'Neill**

fleet of 28 3-cars, 25 4-cars and 10 5-cars will be changed to 21 3-cars, 20 4-cars and 22 6-cars. The new formations had not been confirmed as this book closed for press. The extra vehicles will increase capacity at peak times, particularly on peak-hour trains into Dublin from Kildare, Maynooth/M3 Parkway and Dundalk/Drogheda, as well as on longer distance InterCity services.

The Railcars are normally used in 3-, 4-, 6- or 7-car trains in passenger service, and in formations up to 10-cars for empty stock movements between Laois depot and Dublin. For the 63 units, on Mondays–Thursdays 54 are normally diagrammed for passenger service, 56 on Fridays and Sundays and 55 on Saturdays.

Set numbers (220xx) are not carried but are shown here as each unit is normally referred to by this number.

Seating is 2+2 facing/unidirectional in both Standard and First ("Premier") Class.

Starting in 2019, all units are being refurbished. This includes new leather upholstery and fitting of USB sockets.

There are four different types of vehicles in the 22000s:

221xx or "A1" driving car is formed in the 5-car Premier Class sets only and has 36 First Class seats, a large toilet and buffet counter.

222xx or "A2" driving car is formed in all units apart from the 5-car Premier Class sets and has 66 Standard Class seats and a standard toilet.

223xx or "A3" driving car is formed in all units and has 52 Standard Class seats and a large toilet.

The "B" car is an intermediate vehicle. Each 4-car set has two of these (numbered **225xx** or **228xx** and **224xx**) and each 5-car has three (numbered **227xx, 226xx** and **224xx**). The 228xx cars in 22011–030 have been renumbered from 225xx, 226xx or 227xx cars from the former 6-car sets. All are the same and have 72 Standard Class seats and a standard toilet.

Built: 2007–11 by Hyundai Rotem, Changwon South Korea with bogies and running gear supplied by Mitsui/Tokyu Car Corporation, Japan. 18/8 CrNi stainless steel bodies. Air conditioned.
Wheel arrangement: 2-B + B-2 + B-2 or 2-B + B-2 + B-2 + B-2 or 2-B + B-2 + B-2 + B-2 + B-2.
Engine: One MTU 6H1800 of 360 kW (480 hp) per car.
Length Over Couplers: 23.5 m (end cars), 23.0 m (intermediate vehicles).
Transmission: Hydraulic. Voith T211 re.4. | **Bogies:** Tokyu Car Corporation, Japan.
Width: 2.84 m. | **Wheel Diameter:** 840 mm.
Brakes: Air.
Couplers: Dellner automatic (between units), bar (within unit).
Maximum Speed: 100 mph. | **Home depot:** Laois traincare depot.

†   Fitted with NIR radio, signalling equipment and AWS and TPWS for working into Northern Ireland.
*   Sets 22001 and 22002 are misformed and run semi-permanently coupled as a 6-car set, with vehicles 22202 and 22302 at either end. This is because the cabs of vehicles 22201 and 22301 have been fitted with the prototype IEHS in-cab signalling equipment for trial purposes.
r   refurbished units with new leather upholstery.

3-CAR UNITS
22001–010 delivered 2007–08.
Formation: DMSO–MSO–DMSO.
Accommodation: –/52 1TD 2W + –/72 1T + –/66 1T.
Weight: 49.3 + 47.1 + 49.7 tonnes.

22001	22301	22401	22202	IS	†*r
22002	22302	22402	22201	IS	|*r
22003	22303	22403	22203	IS	†r
22004	22304	22404	22204	IS	†r
22005	22305	22405	22205	IS	†r
22006	22306	22406	22206	IS	†r
22007	22307	22407	22207	IS	r
22008	22308	22408	22208	IS	r
22009	22309	22409	22209	IS	r
22010	22310	22410	22210	IS	r

4-CAR UNITS
22011–030 delivered 2007–08 (originally as 3-car units). Reformed as 4-car units in 2013.
Formation: DMSO–MSO–MSO–DMSO.
Accommodation: –/52 1TD 2W + –/72 1T + –/72 1T + –/66 1T.
Weight: 49.3 + 47.1 + 47.1 + 49.7 tonnes.

22011	22311	22411	22811	22211	**IS**	r	*(22811 renumbered from 22531)*
22012	22312	22412	22812	22212	**IS**		*(22812 renumbered from 22532)*
22013	22313	22413	22813	22213	**IS**		*(22813 renumbered from 22533)*
22014	22314	22414	22814	22214	**IS**	r	*(22814 renumbered from 22534)*
22015	22315	22415	22815	22215	**IS**		*(22815 renumbered from 22535)*
22016	22316	22416	22816	22216	**IS**		*(22816 renumbered from 22536)*
22017	22317	22417	22817	22217	**IS**		*(22817 renumbered from 22537)*
22018	22318	22418	22818	22218	**IS**		*(22818 renumbered from 22538)*
22019	22319	22419	22819	22219	**IS**		*(22819 renumbered from 22539)*
22020	22320	22420	22820	22220	**IS**		*(22820 renumbered from 22540)*
22021	22321	22421	22821	22221	**IS**		*(22821 renumbered from 22641)*
22022	22322	22422	22822	22222	**IS**		*(22822 renumbered from 22741)*
22023	22323	22423	22823	22223	**IS**		*(22823 renumbered from 22642)*
22024	22324	22424	22824	22224	**IS**		*(22824 renumbered from 22742)*
22025	22325	22425	22825	22225	**IS**		*(22825 renumbered from 22643)*
22026	22326	22426	22826	22226	**IS**	r	*(22826 renumbered from 22743)*
22027	22327	22427	22827	22227	**IS**		*(22827 renumbered from 22644)*
22028	22328	22428	22828	22228	**IS**		*(22828 renumbered from 22744)*
22029	22329	22429	22829	22229	**IS**		*(22829 renumbered from 22645)*
22030	22330	22430	22830	22230	**IS**	r	*(22830 renumbered from 22745)*

5-CAR "PREMIER CLASS" UNITS

These ten 5-car sets feature First Class seating with leather upholstery and a buffet car. 22031–040 delivered 2008, originally as 6-car sets (reduced to 5-car units in 2013).

Formation: DMSO–MSO–MSO–DRBFO.
Accommodation: –/52 1TD 2W + –/72 1T + –/72 1T + –/72 1T + 36/– 1TD 1W and buffet.
Weight: 49.3 + 47.1 + 47.3 + 47.1 + 49.8 tonnes.

22031	22331	22431	22631	22731	22131	**IS**	r
22032	22332	22432	22632	22732	22132	**IS**	r
22033	22333	22433	22633	22733	22133	**IS**	r
22034	22334	22434	22634	22734	22134	**IS**	r
22035	22335	22435	22635	22735	22135	**IS**	r
22036	22336	22436	22636	22736	22136	**IS**	†
22037	22337	22437	22637	22737	22137	**IS**	†
22038	22338	22438	22638	22738	22138	**IS**	†r
22039	22339	22439	22639	22739	22139	**IS**	†r
22040	22340	22440	22640	22740	22140	**IS**	

4-CAR UNITS

22041–045 delivered 2009, originally as 6-car sets (reduced to 4-car units in 2013). Details as 22011–030.

22041	22341	22441	22541	22241	**IS**	
22042	22342	22442	22542	22242	**IS**	
22043	22343	22443	22543	22243	**IS**	r
22044	22344	22444	22544	22244	**IS**	
22045	22345	22445	22545	22245	**IS**	

3-CAR UNITS

22046 delivered 2009, 22047–063 delivered 2011–12 as part of the fourth order for 51 additional vehicles.

Formation: DMSO–MSO–DMSO.
Accommodation: –/52 1TD 2W + –/72 1T + –/66 1T.
Weight: 49.4 + 47.1 + 49.7 tonnes.

22046	22346	22446	22246	**IS**	r		22055	22355	22455	22255	**IS**	
22047	22347	22447	22247	**IS**			22056	22356	22456	22256	**IS**	r
22048	22348	22448	22248	**IS**			22057	22357	22457	22257	**IS**	r
22049	22349	22449	22249	**IS**	r		22058	22358	22458	22258	**IS**	
22050	22350	22450	22250	**IS**	r		22059	22359	22459	22259	**IS**	r
22051	22351	22451	22251	**IS**	r		22060	22360	22460	22260	**IS**	r
22052	22352	22452	22252	**IS**	r		22061	22361	22461	22261	**IS**	r
22053	22353	22453	22253	**IS**	r		22062	22362	22462	22262	**IS**	
22054	22354	22454	22254	**IS**	r		22063	22363	22463	22263	**IS**	r

▲ 4-car 22026 and 3-car 22052 stand under the overall roof at Dublin Connolly on 10 September 2019. Both units were operating Commuter services to and from Maynooth.   **Robert Pritchard**

▼ 5-car "Premier Class" 22035 crosses the Curragh, near Kildare with the 07.05 Tralee–Dublin Heuston on 13 September 2019.   **Robert Pritchard**

29000 CLASS   4-CAR OUTER SUBURBAN UNITS

These units are based at Drogheda and mainly work commuter services from Dublin Connolly, Pearse and Docklands to Drogheda/Dundalk (Belfast line), Maynooth/Longford (Sligo line), Gorey (Rosslare line) and to M3 Parkway. There is also a daily turn to Rosslare, peak-hour trains to Bray and booked work to Sligo on Fridays and Sundays for 8-car sets

The first batch of 20 of these units were renumbered (they previously had 4-digit numbers in the 29xx series). Later-build units 29021–029 have detail differences from the earlier members of the class.

Built: 2002–03 (29001–020) and 2005 (29021–029) by CAF, Spain.
Formation: DMSO–MSO–MSO–DMSO.
Wheel Arrangement: B-2 + 2-B + B-2 + 2-B.
Accommodation: –/48 + –/40 (+2) 1TD 2W + –/49 1T + –/48 (2+2 unidirectional/facing).
Weight: 43.56 + 41.36 + 42.07 + 43.52 tonnes.
Engine: One MAN D2876LUH of 294 kW (394 hp) per car.
Transmission: Hydraulic.
Bogies: CAF with coil spring primary suspension and air secondary suspension.
Length Over Couplers: 20.4 m (end cars), 20.2 m (intermediate vehicles).
Width: 2.90 m.
Wheel Diameter: 840 mm.
Brakes: Air.
Couplers: Dellner automatic (between units), bar (within unit).
Maximum Speed: 75 mph.
Home depot: Drogheda.

These units are not fitted with AWS or TPWS for working in Northern Ireland but use north of the border on the "Enterprise" is permitted on an emergency basis to cover for failures of the loco-hauled trains.

Set numbers (290xx) are not carried but are shown here as each unit is normally referred to by this number.

* Sets 29022 and 29029 are misformed and run semi-permanently coupled as an 8-car set, with vehicles 29129 and 29429 at either end. This is because the cabs of vehicles 29122 and 29422 have been fitted with the prototype IEHS in-cab signalling equipment for trial purposes.

29001	29101	29201	29301	29401	G	
29002	29102	29202	29302	29402	C	
29003	29103	29203	29303	29403	G	
29004	29104	29204	29304	29404	C	
29005	29105	29205	29305	29405	G	
29006	29106	29206	29306	29406	C	
29007	29107	29207	29307	29407	G	
29008	29108	29208	29308	29408	C	
29009	29109	29209	29309	29409	G	
29010	29110	29210	29310	29410	C	
29011	29111	29211	29311	29411	C	
29012	29112	29212	29312	29412	G	
29013	29113	29213	29313	29413	C	
29014	29114	29214	29314	29414	G	
29015	29115	29215	29315	29415	G	
29016	29116	29216	29316	29416	C	
29017	29117	29217	29317	29417	G	
29018	29118	29218	29318	29418	C	
29019	29119	29219	29319	29419	G	
29020	29120	29220	29320	29420	G	
29021	29121	29221	29321	29421	G	
29022	29122	29222	29322	29429	C	*
29023	29123	29223	29323	29423	G	
29024	29124	29224	29324	29424	C	
29025	29125	29225	29325	29425	C	
29026	29126	29226	29326	29426	G	
29027	29127	29227	29327	29427	C	
29028	29128	29228	29328	29428	G	
29029	29129	29229	29329	29422	C	*

▲ In the new two-tone green livery unique to this class, 29000 Class 29003 arrives at Broombridge with the 11.40 Maynooth–Dublin Connolly on 11 September 2019.　　**Robert Pritchard**

▼ Still in the original Commuter livery, 29024 passes The Deeps, Killurin, County Wexford with the 13.45 Dublin Connolly–Rosslare Europort on 2 June 2020.　　**Finbarr O'Neill**

1.4. IR ELECTRIC "DART" ROLLING STOCK

These EMUs are used on the frequent "DART" services that operate from Howth or Malahide through Dublin (via Connolly and Pearse) to Bray or Greystones. All seating is 2+2 facing.

Services can run in 2, 4-, 6- or 8-car formations, the normal weekday fleet allocation being 11 x 6-car 8100 Class formations, 6 x 85xx Class 8-car formations and one 85xx Class 4-car formation. This leaves five 8100 Class and four 85xx Class as maintenance spares. Classes 8500/8510/8520 can all operate together.

Home depot: Fairview, Dublin. As Fairview doesn't have a wheel lathe DART sets are hauled to Drogheda or Inchicore for tyre turning (usually by a 29000 Class Railcar).

8100 CLASS   DART 2-CAR UNITS

Original build units. These received a mid-life refurbishment by Siemens in Leipzig, Germany in 2006–08. These units normally work in 6-car formations, but can also work in 4- and 8-car formations. They can operate with the newer units but this only normally happens on empty stock workings. Sets 8110 and 8136 were destroyed by a fire at Fairview depot in 2001 and were scrapped. 8103 was stored in 2010 following extensive fire damage, but was returned to use in 2018.

Built: 1983 by Linke-Hofmann-Busch (LHB) at Salzgitter, West Germany.
System: 1500 V DC overhead.
Formation: DMSO–DTSO.
Wheel Arrangement: Bo-Bo + 2-2.
Accommodation: –/64 1W + –/64 1W.
Weight: 41.58 + 27.87 tonnes.
Traction Motors: 4 GEC G314BY of 137 kW.
Bogies: LHB.
Length Over Couplers: 21.00 + 21.00 m.   **Width:** 2.9 m.
Wheel Diameter: 840 mm.   **Brakes:** Regenerative, Electro-pneumatic and Air.
Couplers: Scharfenberg (between units), bar (within unit).
Maximum Speed: 62 mph.

8101	8301	8112	8312	8122	8322	8131	8331
8102	8302	8113	8313	8123	8323	8132	8332
8103	8303	8114	8314	8124	8324	8133	8333
8104	8304	8115	8315	8125	8325	8134	8334
8105	8305	8116	8316	8126	8326	8135	8335
8106	8306	8117	8317	8127	8327	8137	8337
8107	8307	8118	8318	8128	8328	8138	8338
8108	8308	8119	8319	8129	8329	8139	8339
8109	8309	8120	8320	8130	8330	8140	8340
8111	8311	8121	8321				

8200 CLASS   DART 2-CAR UNITS

These units have been in long-term store since 2006–09. All are stored at Inchicore Works.

Built: 1999–2000 by GEC-Alstom, Santa Perpetua de Mogoda, Spain.
System: 1500 V DC overhead.
Formation: DMSO–DTSO.
Wheel Arrangement: Bo-Bo + 2-2.
Accommodation: –/40 1W + –/40 1W.
Weight: 42.20 + 30.1 tonnes.
Traction Motors: Four Alstom ONYX.
Bogies: Alstom.
Length Over Couplers: 21.17 + 21.17 m.
Width: 2.834 m.
Wheel Diameter: 840 mm.
Brakes: Regenerative, Electro-pneumatic and Air.
Couplers: Scharfenberg (between units), bar (within unit).
Maximum Speed: 62 mph.

8201	8401	(S)	8203	8405	(S)	8204	8404	(S)
8202	8402	(S)						

8205	8403	(S)

▲ 8100 Class 2-car DART sets 8106, 8111 and 8114 stand at Sutton on the Howth branch with the 11.35 Bray–Howth on 10 September 2019. **Robert Pritchard**

▼ 8105 brings up the rear of the 12.35 Bray–Howth at Killester on 10 September 2019 – the train was led by 8120 and 8134. **Robert Pritchard**

8500 CLASS
DART 4-CAR UNITS

Built: 2000 by Tokyu Car Corporation, Yokohama, Japan. Fitted with Richmond high-back seating.
System: 1500 V DC overhead.
Formation: DTSO–PMSO–PMSO–DTSO.
Wheel Arrangement: 2-2 + Bo-Bo + Bo-Bo + 2-2.
Accommodation: –/40 + –/40 + –/40 + –/40. 1W per car.
Weight: 32.70 + 39.00 + 39.00 + 32.70 tonnes.
Traction Motors: Four 3-phase 4-pole squirrel cage AC induction motors.
Bogies: Mitsui TS1024A (motor), TS1025 (trailer).
Length Over Couplers: 20.73 + 20.50 + 20.50 + 20.73 m.
Width: 2.9 m.   **Wheel Diameter:** 840 mm.
Brakes: Regenerative, Electro-pneumatic and Air.
Couplers: Scharfenberg (between units), bar (within unit).   **Maximum Speed:** 62 mph.

8601	8501	8502	8602		8605	8505	8506	8606
8603	8503	8504	8604		8607	8507	8508	8608

8510 CLASS
DART 4-CAR UNITS

Built: 2001 by Tokyu Car Corporation, Yokohama, Japan. Fitted with Richmond high-back seating.
System: 1500 V DC overhead.
Formation: DTSO–PMSO–PMSO–DTSO.
Wheel Arrangement: 2-2 + Bo-Bo + Bo-Bo + 2-2.
Accommodation: –/40 + –/40 + –/40 + –/40. 1W per car.
Weight: 34.46 + 39.70 + 39.70 + 34.21 tonnes.
Traction Motors: Four 3-phase 4-pole squirrel cage AC induction motors.
Bogies: Mitsui TS1024A (motor), TS1025A (trailer).
Length Over Couplers: 20.73 + 20.50 + 20.50 + 20.73 m.
Width: 2.9 m.   **Wheel Diameter:** 840 mm.
Brakes: Regenerative, Electro-pneumatic and Air.
Couplers: Scharfenberg (between units), bar (within unit).   **Maximum Speed:** 62 mph.

8611	8511	8512	8612		8615	8515	8516	8616
8613	8513	8514	8614					

8520 CLASS
DART 4-CAR UNITS

Built: 2003–04 by Tokyu Car Corporation, Yokohama, Japan. Fitted with air conditioning and a new design of high-back seating.
System: 1500 V DC overhead.
Formation: DTSO–PMSO–PMSO–DTSO.
Wheel Arrangement: 2-2 + Bo-Bo + Bo-Bo + 2-2.
Accommodation: –/40 + –/40 + –/40 + –/40. 1W per car.
Weight: 32.70 + 39.00 + 39.00 + 32.70 tonnes.
Traction Motors: Four 3-phase 4-pole squirrel cage AC induction motors.
Bogies: Mitsui TS1024B (motor), TS1025B (trailer).
Length Over Couplers: 20.73 + 20.50 + 20.50 + 20.73 m.
Width: 2.9 m.
Wheel Diameter: 840 mm.
Brakes: Regenerative, Electro-pneumatic and Air.
Couplers: Scharfenberg (between units), bar (within unit).
Maximum Speed: 62 mph.

*   Sets 8621 and 8625 are misformed and run semi-permanently coupled as an 8-car set, with vehicles 8621 and 8622 at either end. This is because the cabs of vehicles 8625 and 8626 have been fitted with the prototype IEHS in-cab signalling equipment for trial purposes.

8621	8521	8526	8626	*	8631	8531	8532	8632	
8623	8523	8524	8624		8633	8533	8534	8634	
8625	8525	8522	8622	*	8635	8535	8536	8636	
8627	8527	8528	8628		8637	8537	8538	8638	
8629	8529	8530	8630		8639	8539	8540	8640	

▲ 8500/8520 Class sets 8602/01+8635/36 leave Seapoint with the 15.25 Bray–Malahide on 11 September 2019. **Robert Pritchard**

▼ The misformed and semi-permanently coupled 8520 Class set 8621/26+8625/22 arrives at Raheny with the 10.34 Greystones–Malahide on 10 September 2019. **Robert Pritchard**

2. TRANSLINK NORTHERN IRELAND RAILWAYS

GENERAL

The railways in Northern Ireland are operated by the Province's nationalised transport operator, Translink under the banner of "Translink Northern Ireland Railways".

LIVERIES

NIR locomotives are painted in the company's blue livery. Older Railcars (80 and 450 Class) were painted in the Translink livery of white and blue with a green band under the windows. 3000 and 4000 Class Railcars work all scheduled services and are painted in a revised Translink silver and blue livery.

▲ Northern Ireland Railways operates two similar types of diesel unit. Showing the comparison in front ends, on 14 September 4005 and 3007 stand at Whitehead. **Robert Pritchard**

2.1. NIR DIESEL LOCOMOTIVES

111 CLASS   Co-Co

These locos are almost identical to the Irish Rail 071 Class and were employed on the Belfast–Dublin service before the De Dietrich stock and 201s were introduced. They are now used on infrastructure trains as required across the NIR network.

Built: 1980 (8111/112) and 1984 (8113) by General Motors, La Grange, Illinois, USA.
Engine: General Motors 12-cylinder 645 E3B two stroke, turbocharged developing of 1830 kW (2450 hp) gross at 900 rpm with 1675 kW (2250 hp) available for traction.
Transmission: Electric. 6 axle-hung nose-suspended General Motors D77B traction motors.
Maximum Tractive Effort: 245 kN (55 100 lbf).
Continuous Tractive Effort: 210 kN (47 200 lbf) at 15.1 mph
Power At Rail: 1360 kW (1825 hp).
Weight: 99 tonnes.
Length Over Buffers: 17.37 m.
Wheel Diameter: 1016 mm.
Train Brakes: Air and Vacuum.
Multiple Working: With GM locomotives.
Maximum Speed: 90 mph.

8111	GREAT NORTHERN
8112	NORTHERN COUNTIES
8113	BELFAST & COUNTY DOWN

201 CLASS   Co-Co

For details of the two locos owned by Translink for the jointly-operated Belfast–Dublin service (8208 and 8209) see the Irish Rail section.

▲ 111 Class 8113 arrives at Dundalk with the RPSI's Mark 2 set on 20 October 2013 with the 09.45 Whitehead–Dundalk "Across the Tracks" RPSI railtour.   **Finbarr O'Neill**

2.2. NIR DIESEL RAILCARS

3000 CLASS   3-CAR UNITS

The 23 3000 Class Railcars are used in 3- and 6-car formations on all routes across the country – from Belfast to Londonderry, Portrush, Larne Harbour, Bangor and Portadown/Newry. Air conditioned.

Built: 2004–05 by CAF, Zaragoza, Spain.
Formation: DMSO–MSO–DMSO.
Wheel arrangement: 2-B + 2-B + B-2.
Accommodation: –/49 (+9) 1TD 2W + –/78 + –/58 (+6) 1T.
Weight: 49.5 + 45.5 + 49.2 tonnes.
Engine: MAN D2876 LUH 03 of 338 kW (453 hp) per car.
Auxiliary engine: Cummins 6BT5.9-GR1, providing 71 kW (95 hp) per car.
Transmission: Hydraulic. Voith.   **Bogies:** CAF.
Length Over Couplers: 23.74 + 23.14 + 23.74 m.   **Width:** 2.76 m.
Wheel diameter: 864 mm.   **Brakes:** Air.
Couplers: Scharfenberg automatic (unit ends), Scharfenberg semi-permanent (within unit).
Maximum Speed: 90 mph.

*   Fitted with CAWS and Irish Rail train radio for use on cross-border services if required.

3001	3301	3501	3401	*	3013	3313	3513	3413
3002	3302	3502	3402	*	3014	3314	3514	3414
3003	3303	3503	3403	*	3015	3315	3515	3415
3004	3304	3504	3404	*	3016	3316	3516	3416
3005	3305	3505	3405	*	3017	3317	3517	3417
3006	3306	3506	3406	*	3018	3318	3518	3418
3007	3307	3507	3407		3019	3319	3519	3419
3008	3308	3508	3408		3020	3320	3520	3420
3009	3309	3509	3409		3021	3321	3521	3421
3010	3310	3510	3410		3022	3322	3522	3422
3011	3311	3511	3411		3023	3323	3523	3423
3012	3312	3512	3412					

▲ 3000 Class 3003 leaves Belfast Great Victoria Street with the 09.55 Bangor–Lisburn on 14 September 2019.   **Robert Pritchard**

▲ An unidentified 3000 Class unit is seen between Castlerock and Downhill Tunnels on the stunning coastal section of the Londonderry line on 18 September 2019, operating the 13.10 Belfast Great Victoria Street–Londonderry. **Finbarr O'Neill**

4000 CLASS   3-CAR UNITS

The 20 4000 Class Railcars were introduced in 2011–12 and are similar to the 3000s, the main difference being the MTU/ZF traction package compared to MAN/Voith package used in the 3000s. The elimination of a separate auxiliary power unit makes the 4000s slightly lighter. These units also work across all NIR routes but have not been cleared for cross-border operation. The 4000s also work in 6-car formations but the 3000s and 4000s do not work together in passenger service. Air conditioned.

In December 2018 an additional 21 4000 Class intermediate vehicles were ordered. These will be delivered in 2021–22 to augment sets 4014–20 to 6-cars to enabled more 6-car operation at peak times. The planned new formations have now been confirmed, with the additional vehicles shown here in italics. The 48xx vehicle is planned to include a universal access toilet.

Built: 2010–12 by CAF, Zaragoza, Spain. Centre cars for 4014–20 2020–21 by CAF, Zaragoza, Spain.
Formation: DMSO–MSO–DMSO or DMSO–MSO–MSO–MSO–MSO–DMSO.
Wheel arrangement: 2-B + 2-B + B-2 (6-car to be confirmed).
Accommodation: –/61 (+10) + –/56 (+14) 1TD 2W + –/61 (+10) (6-cars to be confirmed).
Weight: 48.1 + 46.5 + 47.9 tonnes (6-car to be confirmed).
Engine: MTU 6H1800R84 of 390 kW (520 hp) per car.
Transmission: Mechanical. ZF 5HP902.
Bogies: CAF.
Length Over Couplers: 23.74 + 23.14 + 23.74 m.   **Width:** 2.76 m.
Wheel diameter: 864 mm.   **Brakes:** Air.
Couplers: Scharfenberg automatic (unit ends), Scharfenberg semi-permanent (within unit).
Maximum Speed: 90 mph.

3-CAR UNITS

4001–13 will remain as 3-car units as-built.

4001	4301	4501	4401		4008	4308	4508	4408
4002	4302	4502	4402		4009	4309	4509	4409
4003	4303	4503	4403		4010	4310	4510	4410
4004	4304	4504	4404		4011	4311	4511	4411
4005	4305	4505	4405		4012	4312	4512	4412
4006	4306	4506	4406		4013	4313	4513	4413
4007	4307	4507	4407					

3-CAR UNITS (from 2021–22 6-CAR UNITS)

4014–20 built as 3-cars, to be augmented to 6-cars during 2021–22. Planned additional vehicles are shown in *italics*.

4014	4314	4514	*4614*	*4714*	*4814*	4414
4015	4315	4515	*4615*	*4715*	*4815*	4415
4016	4316	4516	*4616*	*4716*	*4816*	4416
4017	4317	4517	*4617*	*4717*	*4817*	4417
4018	4318	4518	*4618*	*4718*	*4818*	4418
4019	4319	4519	*4619*	*4719*	*4819*	4419
4020	4320	4520	*4620*	*4720*	*4820*	4420

▲ The state-of-the-art depot at Adelaide was built to accommodate the new 4000 Class units. On 13 March 2014 4008 and 4020 are seen undergoing maintenance. **Robert Pritchard**

▼ 4010 arrives at City Hospital, one of two stations between Belfast's two main stations (Great Victoria Street and Lanyon Place) with the 11.40 Lisburn–Bangor on 14 September 2019. **Robert Pritchard**

3. IR/NIR JOINT STOCK FOR THE "ENTERPRISE" SERVICE

This stock is used on the Belfast–Dublin cross-border "Enterprise" service. Built to work as four push-pull sets but later reformed as three 8-car sets with an extra Open Standard and one spare vehicle of each type. However, sets now normally run with seven passenger coaches (plus one generator van) meaning there are four spare Open Standards and one spare of each other type of coach. In 2011–12 four redundant Irish Rail Mark 3 Electric Generating Vans were refurbished and brought into use to provide power to avoid the need for the 201 locomotives to provide the sometimes unreliable Head End Power (HEP).

The coaches were refurbished at York Road, Belfast as part of a £12.2 million project in 2014–16. The remodelled interiors were PRM compliant with retrimmed seats and new tables, at-seat power sockets, a new Train Management System and "traffic light" seat reservation system. The eight bench seats in the catering car were replaced by 15 seats in a 2+1 layout for use by Standard Class passengers dining.

Formations are normally Locomotive (at the Belfast end)–Electric Generating Van–4 x Open Standard (one with wheelchair space)–Catering Car–Open First–Driving Trailer. The coaches are maintained by Translink at York Road, Belfast.

As part of the Enterprise service being jointly operated by Irish Rail and Translink Northern Ireland Railways, IR owns the odd numbered coaches and NIR the even numbered coaches, and all four of the Mark 3 Electric Generating Vans.

Livery: All coaches carry the new Enterprise (**EN**) livery.

DRIVING TRAILER BRAKE OPEN FIRST

Built: 1996 by De Dietrich, Reichshoffen, France. Gangwayed at one end only.
Accommodation: 29/– (+2) 1T.   **Heating System:** Air conditioning.
Brakes: Air.   **Bogies:** DDF.
Weight: 39.7 tonnes.   **Length over buffers:** 23.00 m.
Width: 2.85 m.   **Gangway:** Heubner, Germany.
Couplers: Dellner (inner end); Drop-head buckeye (outer end).
Maximum Speed: 100 mph.

| 9001 | 9002 | 9003 | 9004 |

▲ Enterprise Driving Trailer Brake Open First 9004 brings up the rear of the 09.30 Dublin Connolly–Belfast Lanyon Place at City Hospital on 14 September 2019 as 3023 arrives.   **Robert Pritchard**

OPEN FIRST

Built: 1996 by De Dietrich, Reichshoffen, France.
Accommodation: 47/– 1T.
Brakes: Air.
Weight: 37.7 tonnes.
Width: 2.85 m.
Maximum Speed: 100 mph.

Heating System: Air conditioning.
Bogies: DDF.
Length over buffers: 23.00 m.
Couplers: Dellner.
Gangways: Heubner, Germany.

| 9101 | 9102 | 9103 | 9104 |

OPEN STANDARD

Built: 1996 by De Dietrich, Reichshoffen, France.
Accommodation: –/71 1T (* –/68 1TD 1W).
Heating System: Air conditioning.
Brakes: Air.
Weight: 37.5 tonnes.
Width: 2.85 m.
Maximum Speed: 100 mph

Bogies: DDF.
Length over buffers: 23.00 m.
Couplers: Dellner.
Gangways: Heubner, Germany.

9201	9205	9209	9213	*
9202	9206	9210	9214	*
9203	9207	9211	9215	*
9204	9208	9212	9216	*

CATERING CAR

Built: 1996 by De Dietrich, Reichshoffen, France. Vehicle with kitchen and buffet counter.
Accommodation: –/15.
Brakes: Air.
Weight: 38.0 tonnes.
Width: 2.85 m.
Maximum Speed: 100 mph.

Heating System: Air conditioning.
Bogies: DDF.
Length over buffers: 23.00 m.
Couplers: Dellner.
Gangways: Heubner, Germany.

| 9401 | 9402 | 9403 | 9404 |

MARK 3 ELECTRIC GENERATING VANS

Built: 7604/05 1984–86 by BREL at Derby Carriage & Wagon Works, with finishing carried out by CIÉ at Inchicore Works. 7608/13 1986–88 by CIÉ/IR at Inchicore Works. All to BR Mark 3 design.
Accommodation: no seats.
Engine: Two Cummins of 220 kW (295 hp).
Brakes: Air.
Weight: 35.60 tonnes.
Width: 2.74 m.
Maximum Speed: 100 mph.

Bogies: BT22.
Length over buffers: 23.00 m.
Couplers: Dellner.
Gangways: Non-gangwayed.

| 9602 (7604) | 9604 (7605) | 9606 (7608) | 9608 (7613) |

▲ Enterprise Open First 9104 at Raheny on 10 September 2019. **Robert Pritchard**

▼ Enterprise Electric Generating Van 9602 is seen at City Hospital on 14 September 2019.
Robert Pritchard

4. THE BELMOND GRAND HIBERNIAN LUXURY TRAIN

The Belmond Grand Hibernian luxury train was launched in August 2016. It is operated by Belmond and is usually hauled by an Irish Rail 201 Class loco (normally 216, still owned by IR but painted in Grand Hibernian blue livery) and a rake of ten Mark 3 coaches that were purchased by Belmond from Irish Rail and extensively rebuilt. An 071 Class loco is booked to work the Dublin–Waterford and return leg.

Irish Rail is contracted to operate the train. Although the train was not expected to operate at all in 2020 because of the coronavirus pandemic, it normally operates to a weekly schedule between April and October, including a four-night tour of the Republic of Ireland (Dublin–Cork–Killarney–Galway–Westport–Dublin)) and then a two-night weekend trip including a visit to Belfast (Dublin–Belfast–Dublin–Waterford–Dublin). With Monday the allocated day for maintenance at Inchicore, each week starts on a Tuesday, the full schedule normally being as follows:

Tuesday:
14.25 Dublin Heuston–Cork 17.02
20.35 Cork–Charleville 21.17
Wednesday:
07.45 Charleville–Mallow 08.05
08.37 Mallow–Cork 09.02
12.55 Cork–Killarney 15.02
Thursday:
07.00 Killarney–Galway 13.13
18.35 Galway–Athlone 21.03
Friday:
06.15 Athlone–Westport 08.40
18.45 Westport–Roscommon 21.20

Saturday:
06.15 Roscommon–Dublin Heuston 08.50
12.10 Dublin Heuston–Belfast Lanyon Place 16.15
20.26 Belfast Lanyon Place–Dundalk 21.55
Sunday:
08.20 Dundalk–Dublin Connolly 09.35
10.05 Dublin Connolly–Waterford 13.25
19.10 Waterford–Muine Bheag 20.35
Monday:
08.00 Muine Bheag–Dublin Heuston 10.05

Carriages used were built by BREL for Irish Rail between 1984 and 1988 and withdrawn by Irish Rail in 2008–09. They were refurbished (including a mechanical overhaul and repaint) at a cost of £7 million by Assenta Ltd at Brodie's, Kilmarnock, with internal fitting out carried out by Mivan Marine Ltd in Antrim, Northern Ireland. The coaches include five sleeping cars, two restaurant cars, an observation car plus an Electric Generating Van. The complete train provides 20 en-suite cabins with accomodation for 40 passengers.

Each carriage has been repainted into dark blue livery and given the name of an Irish county.

Rebuilt from Mark 3 Open Standard, Open First, Open Composite or Electric Generating Van:

Belmond No.	Former IR No.	Description	Converted from	Name
87001	7116	Sleeping Car	Open Standard	FERMANAGH
87002	7158	Sleeping Car	Open Standard	LEITRIM
87003	7129	Sleeping Car	Open Standard	WATERFORD
87004	7149	Sleeping Car	Open Standard	DOWN
87005	7137	Sleeping Car	Open Standard	KERRY
87101	7171	Dining Car	Open Composite	SLIGO
87102	7169	Dining Car	Open Composite	WEXFORD
87103	7104	Observation Car	Open First	KILDARE
87104	7601	Generator Car	Electric Generating Van	CARLOW
87110	7130	Crew Accommodation Car	Open Standard	DONEGAL

Stored Belmond vehicles
7122   Inchicore Works (former Open Standard)

▲ Dedicated Belmond loco 216 passes Ballyhillogue, between Mallow and Cork, with the launch train of the first full Grand Hibernian season in 2017, running as the 14.20 Dublin Heuston–Cork on 25 April 2017. **Finbarr O'Neill**

▼ Grand Hibernian Observation Car 87103 "KILDARE" (the former Irish Rail 7104) is seen at Ballyhillogue on 25 April 2017. **Finbarr O'Neill**

5. ON-TRACK MACHINES

On-Track Machines operated by Irish Rail and Northern Ireland Railways are listed below. The main maintenance base for IR machines is the depot at Kildare, where several machines can normally be found. Other stabling and servicing points include the permanent way depot at Portlaoise and the yard alongside the station at Limerick Junction. In Northern Ireland the main base for OTMs is at Ballymena, whilst machines may also be found at smaller depots at Coleraine and Lisburn. Note that not all of the Northern Ireland machines carry their 70xx series number, and some carry no number at all!

5.1. IRISH RAIL ON-TRACK MACHINES

No.	Type	Description	Notes
700	Plasser & Theurer EM 50	Track Recording Car	
701	Geismar Track Recording Vehicle	Track Recording Vehicle	Delivered to IR in 2020
703	Plasser & Theurer USP 4000	Ballast Regulator	
704	Plasser & Theurer USP 4000	Ballast Regulator	
710	Plasser & Theurer DTS 62N	Dynamic Track Stabiliser	
721	Hugh Phillips Engineering HPE 370	Inspection Car	
722	Matisa VM100ST	Inspection Car	
723	Matisa VM100ST	Inspection Car	
739	Plasser & Theurer 08-16 SP-4	Tamper	
740	Plasser & Theurer 09-16 CAT-5	Tamper	(S) Cork
741	Plasser & Theurer 09-16 CAT DYMANIC	Tamper	
742	Plasser & Theurer 08-16 4x4	Tamper	
743	Plasser & Theurer 08-16 4x4	Tamper	
744	Plasser & Theurer 09-2X	Tamper	
751	Plasser & Theurer 08-4x4/4S	Tamper	
780	Plasser & Theurer RM76 UHR	Ballast Cleaner	(S) Limerick Junction
781	Plasser & Theurer RM90	Ballast Cleaner	
790	Geismar MPV	Multi Purpose Vehicle	

5.2. NORTHERN IRELAND RAILWAYS ON-TRACK MACHINES

No.	Type	Description	Notes
7005	Plasser & Theurer MU07-16	Tamper	(S) Ballymena PW depot
7008	Plasser & Theurer MU08-16 SPT	Tamper	Carries No. "08 N°8"
7009	Plasser & Theurer 08-16/4x4 4C80RT	Tamper	Carries No. "DR 73926"*
7010	Plasser & Theurer USP 5000RT	Ballast Regulator	Carries no number
7015	Plasser & Theurer K355-APT	Welding Machine	Carries no number
7017	Geismar VMT 850 GR	Formation Repair Machine	Carries no number
NI 11	Windoff MPV	Multi Purpose Vehicle	Carries 99 70 9428 011-9

*   Not to be confused with the British Tamper that carries the same number.

▲ Irish Rail Plasser & Theurer EM 50 Track Recording Car 700 is seen at the On-Track Machine depot at Kildare on 13 September 2019.
Robert Pritchard

▼ Irish Rail Plasser & Theurer 09-2X Tamper 744 is seen stabled at Killarney on 3 July 2020.
Neil Dinnen

▲ Irish Rail Geismar Multi Purpose Vehicle 790 is seen at Kildare on 13 September 2019.
Robert Pritchard

▼ Northern Ireland Railways Plasser & Theurer MU08-16 SPT Tamper 7008 is seen stabled in the centre road at Bangor on 13 March 2014. **Robert Pritchard**

6. LUAS – DUBLIN LIGHT RAIL SYSTEM

Following the introduction of horse trams in 1872, an electric tram system operated in Dublin between 1901 and 1949. At its height there were 60 route miles. Plans to reintroduce trams to the city were approved in May 1998, with construction of the first line starting in October 2000. The two separate routes both opened in 2004. Since then there have been four extensions to these routes, the latest being in December 2017. The system was called "Luas", which means "Speed" in Irish, and the two routes are differentiated by colours: Green and Red. Unlike the Irish railway system, Luas was built to the European standard gauge of 4 ft 8½ in (1435 mm).

Luas has been operated by Transdev since 2011 (previously it was operated by Connex and then Veolia, who merged with Transdev in 2011). In June 2019 Transdev won a new contract to continue to operate and maintain Luas from 2019 until 2025.

The first section to open was the Green Line from St Stephen's Green, at the top of one of the main shopping districts (Grafton Street) to Sandyford. Much of this route was constructed on the old Harcourt Street–Bray railway line, featuring segregated railway style alignments and a number of impressive viaducts. This line was extended to Brides Glen, through some attractive countryside, in 2010.

The Red Line also opened in 2004, linking the two main Dublin city centre stations (Connolly and Heuston) with the south-west of the city. The Red Line has long sections following roads, mainly in central reserved space, with priority at junctions. Extensions followed to The Point (Docklands) and Saggart.

The three extensions that opened in 2009–11 focussed on serving in-hand or future housing or office developments, with contributions from developers financing the projects. However some of the proposed developments were halted by the recession and these extensions have operated at well below capacity. Two stops on the Green Line Brides Glen extension (Racecourse and Brennanstown) were constructed but are not yet open as they have no access roads.

A line to Broombridge, part of the originally planned Luas system but dropped in favour of a Metro North rail line, opened on 9 December 2017. This saw the Green Line extended through Dublin city centre and the two self-contained lines finally connected, although the connections are only booked to be used by empty stock movements between the two lines. A second, smaller, Green Line depot was constructed alongside the terminus at Broombridge.

The new Broombridge lines uses part of the old Broadstone railway in north Dublin, with the terminus being alongside the Irish Rail station. A one way system operates in the city centre, with northbound trams crossing the river on one bridge and then crossing the Red Line to the west of the Abbey Street stop and heading down O'Connell Street. At O'Connell trams can either continue to Broombridge or turn right to Parnell and return to the city centre towards St Stephen's Green. From Parnell trams run down Marlborough Street to cross the Red Line just east of the Abbey Street stop, rejoining the other line at Trinity.

On the Green Line most trams heading into the city centre from Brides Glen and Sandyford "turn right" at O'Connell Upper to Parnell and then return south via Marlborough. These trams display "Parnell" as their destination. The off-peak pattern does vary on an hour-by-hour basis as the peak and off-peak timetable steps up or down. A typical middle-of-the-day hour will see five trams from Brides Glen to Parnell and five trams from Sandyford to Broombridge. The longest possible journey, Brides Glen–Broombridge (1h7) mainly just runs at peak times on weekdays. At peak times there are additional trams from both Brides Glen and Sandyford. Saturdays generally see four departures every hour from Brides Glen and four from Sandyford. Sundays see the most straightforward service with all trams running throughout from Brides Glen to Broombridge every 12 minutes from 10.30 to 20.30 and less frequently at other times.

On the Red Line, during the day, there are eight departures per hour from The Point, four to Tallaght and four to Saggart. In addition, there are four departures per hour from Connolly, two to Tallaght and two to Saggart. These combine to give a tram roughly every five minutes on the core Busáras–Belgard section. Additional peak-hour trams operate to and from Tallaght and there are also some peak services that operate as a Heuston–Connolly shuttle. The Point–Saggart is the longest journey at 55 minutes. A broadly similar service operates on Saturdays and on Sundays trams operate The Point–Tallaght every ten minutes, with Connolly–Heuston shuttles every 20 minutes in the afternoon. Belgard–Saggart is operated as a self-contained branch all day on Sundays. Full timetables for both lines can be found on the National Transport Authority's journey planner site: www.journeyplanner.transportforireland.ie.

The Luas fleet comprises Alstom Citadis low-floor bi-directional trams of aluminium construction. When the first of these trams were delivered in 2003 they were the first of this type of tram for a city outside of France. Types 301, 401 and 402 have four bogies – three power bogies and one trailer bogie and type 502 has five bogies, four power and one trailer. Alstom maintains the trams at the Red Cow, Sandyford and Broombridge depots.

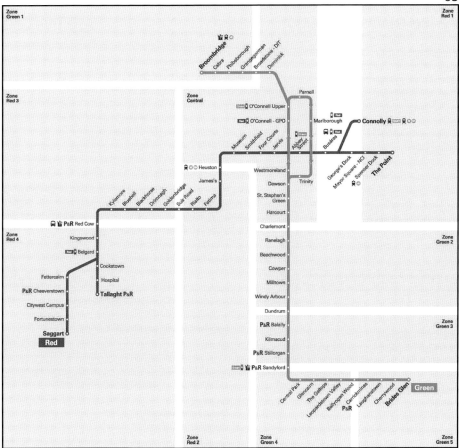

▲ Luas current network map also showing the fare zones.

Luas route opening dates and mileages

Route	Opening date	Length
St Stephen's Green–Sandyford (Green Line)	June 2004	5.6 miles
Connolly–Tallaght (Red Line)	September 2004	9.4 miles
Busáras/Connolly*–The Point (Red Line)	December 2009	1 mile
Sandyford–Brides Glen (Green Line)	October 2010	4.7 miles
Belgard–Saggart (Red Line)	July 2011	2.6 miles
St Stephen's Green–Broombridge (Green Line)	December 2017	3.6 miles

* There is a triangle between Busáras and Connolly enabling trams to run direct from Connolly to The Point, but there are no scheduled services that run this way.

ALSTOM CITADIS TYPE TGA301   5-SECTION CARS

Used on the Red Line. These cars were built as 30 m cars but later extended to 40 m cars (to become essentially identical to the Type 401 cars). 80% low floor.

Built: 2002–03 (extra centre sections 2007–08).   **Builder:** Alstom, La Rochelle, France.
Wheel arrangement: Bo+Bo+2+Bo.
Traction motors: 4 x 140 kW 3-phase AC asynchronous.
Bogies: Outer power bogies: Magdeburg LHB type.
       Inner power bogies: Arpege Motor type:
       Trailer bogie: Arpege Trailer type.
Accommodation: 72 + 8 tip up seats.
Length: 40.8 m.   **Width:** 2.40 m.
Weight: 50.0 tonnes.   **Maximum speed:** 70 km/h.

†   At the time of writing these trams are on loan to the Green Line.

Advertising Liveries:
3019   Lidl (blue & red). | 3021   Tesco (white).

3001	3006	3011	3015	3019 AL	3023
3002	3007	3012	3016	3020 †	3024 †
3003	3008	3013	3017	3021 AL	3025
3004	3009	3014	3018	3022	3026
3005	3010				

ALSTOM CITADIS TYPE TGA401   5-SECTION CARS

Used on the Red Line. These cars were initially used on the Green Line, but transferred to the Red Line when the Type 402 cars were introduced. 80% low floor.

Built: 2002–03.   **Builder:** Alstom, La Rochelle, France.
Wheel arrangement: Bo+Bo+2+Bo.
Traction motors: 4 x 140 kW 3-phase AC asynchronous.
Bogies: Outer power bogies: Magdeburg LHB type.
       Inner power bogies: Arpege Motor type:
       Trailer bogie: Arpege Trailer type.
Accommodation: 72 + 8 tip up seats.
Length: 40.8 m.   **Width:** 2.40 m.
Weight: 50.0 tonnes.   **Maximum speed:** 70 km/h.

†   At the time of writing these trams are on loan to the Green Line.

4001 †	4004	4007	4009	4011	4013
4002	4005	4008	4010	4012 †	4014 †
4003	4006				

ALSTOM CITADIS TYPE TGA402 or TGA502   7-SECTION OR 9-SECTION CARS

Used on the Green Line. 5001–26 were built with seven shorter sections compared to the five sections of the earlier cars. A restyled front end nose gives a higher level of crashworthiness and the cars are also 100% low floor. 5027–33 were delivered in 2017–18 to cover the requirement for additional trams for the Broombridge extension: these are 54.6 m trams, with nine sections. Between autumn 2019 and the end of 2020 cars 5001–26 are being extended to nine sections and in addition eight further new 9-section trams are being delivered during 2020–21 (numbered 5034–41) to allow additional peak-hour services to operate and also allow the five trams on loan from the Red Line trams to be returned. The first lengthened car, 5021, entered service in September 2019 and the first of the next batch of trams, 5034, arrived in July 2020.

Built: 2008–10; cars 5027–41 and extra centre sections 2017–21.
Builder: Alstom, La Rochelle, France.
Wheel arrangement: TGA402: Bo+Bo+2+Bo; TGA502: Bo+Bo+2+Bo+Bo.
Traction motors: TGA402: 6 x 120 kW 3-phase AC asynchronous; TGA502: 8 x 120 kW 3-phase AC asynchronous.
Bogies: Power bogies: Arpege 360M 1600 type.
       Trailer bogies: Arpege 360P 1600 type.
Accommodation: TGA402: 70 + 8 tip-up seats; TGA502: 88 + 8 tip-up seats.
Overall Length: 43.5 m or 54.6 m.   **Width:** 2.40 m.
Weight: 51.5 or ?? tonnes.   **Maximum speed:** 70 km/h.

Advertising Livery:
5003   Tesco (white).

Type TGA402 7-section trams (* lengthened to 9-sections as type TGA502):

5001	*	5006	*	5011		5015		5019		5023
5002	*	5007		5012	*	5016		5020	*	5024
5003	* AL	5008	*	5013		5017		5021	*	5025
5004	*	5009	*	5014	*	5018	*	5022		5026
5005		5010	*							

Type TGA502 built as 9-section trams. 5034–41 are due for delivery 2020–21.

5027	5030	5033	5036	5038	5040
5028	5031	5034	5037	5039	5041
5029	5032	5035			

General information
Route miles: 26.9 miles.
Number of stops: Red Line: 32.   Green Line: 35.
Depots: Red Line: Red Cow.   Green Line: Sandyford and Broombridge.
Control Centre (both lines): Red Cow.
System: 750 V DC overhead.
Passenger numbers: 48.1 million in 2019 (up from 22.2M in 2005, the first full year of operation). Annual growth was more than 15% compared to 2018.
Hours of operation (from departure of first tram to arrival of last tram): Mondays–Fridays 04.55–01.20; Saturdays 06.10–01.20; Sundays and Bank Holidays 06.30–00.20.
Tickets: In 2020 ticket prices started at €2.10 for a single in Zone 1 to €7.30 for a day ticket covering both lines. The Dublin "Leap" smartcard is valid on Luas and offers savings for those making regular journeys.
Trams per route: Red Line: 35. Green Line: 38 (includes five on hire from the Red Line), plus 8 on order.
Livery: Silver with a yellow stripe and black window surrounds. (**AL** = Advertising livery).

▲ Type TGA301 car **3015** stands outside Dublin Heuston station with a Red Line service to The Point on the late evening of 10 September 2019.   **Robert Pritchard**

▲ The point at which the single track Green Line (heading south) crosses the Red Line on Abbey Street. 5004 is heading to Brides Glen and 3002 stands at the Abbey Street stop with a service for Connolly on 10 September 2019. Another Red Line tram heads towards Heuston.   **Robert Pritchard**

▼ The Broombridge terminus is alongside the Irish Rail station on the Maynooth/Sligo line. On 11 September 2019 5012 awaits departure with a service to Sandyford.   **Robert Pritchard**

▲ 5019 leaves the Broadstone – DIT stop on the new Broombridge line with a service for Sandyford on 11 September 2019. The building behind the tram is the former Broadstone railway station, the Dublin terminus of the Midland Great Western Railway of Ireland (closed to passenger services in 1937) and now used as the headquarters for Bus Éireann. **Robert Pritchard**

▼ One of the latest batch of 5000 series (type TGA502) 9-section cars, 5033, leaves Harcourt with a service for Broombridge on 11 September 2019. **Robert Pritchard**

7. PRESERVED LOCOMOTIVES & RAILCARS

In this section, the following status codes are used:

M   Museum, on display (non-operational).
MA   Museum, active.
MM   Museum, active (registered for use on the main line).
MR   Museum, under repair or overhaul.
MS   Museum, stored.
P   Plinthed.
S   Stored.

7.1. STANDARD GAUGE STEAM LOCOMOTIVES

7.1.1. Ex-GSR/CIÉ

GREAT SOUTHERN & WESTERN RAILWAY

CLASS 23   2-2-2

Built: 1847 by Bury, Curtis & Kennedy, Liverpool.
Boiler Pressure: 80 lbf/sq in.
Cylinders: 15 x 20 in.
Driving Wheel Diameter: 6 ft 0 in.   **Tractive Effort:** 4250 lbf.
Weight: 22 tons 19 cwt.

36		P	Cork Station	Bury 1847

CLASS J30   0-6-0T

Built: 1875 by LNWR at Crewe. Originally built as a 0-6-4WT steam railmotor.
Boiler Pressure: 150 lbf/sq in.
Cylinders: 10 x 18 in.
Driving Wheel Diameter: 3 ft 6 in.   **Tractive Effort:** 7425 lbf.
Weight: 22 tons 9 cwt.   **Valve Gear:** Stephenson.

On loan from Irish Rail to the Downpatrick & County Down Railway.

90		MA	Downpatrick & County Down Railway	Crewe 1875

CLASS J15   0-6-0

Built: 1879–80. This was by far the most numerous class of locomotive (steam or diesel) ever to run in Ireland: 111 were built between 1866 and 1903, the majority by the GS&WR at Inchicore, although some were sub-contracted to Beyer Peacock & Co and Sharp Stewart & Co in Manchester.
Boiler Pressure: 160 lbf/sq in.
Cylinders: 18 x 24 in.
Driving Wheel Diameter: 5 ft 2 in.   **Tractive Effort:** 17170 lbf.
Weight: 37 tons 13 cwt.   **Valve Gear:** Stephenson.

GSWR	GSR/CIÉ			
184	184	MS	RPSI, Whitehead	Inchicore 1880
186	186	MS	RPSI, Whitehead	SS 2838/1879

▲ 1847-built Great Southern & Western Railway 2-2-2 No. 36 is on permanent display on the main station concourse of Cork Kent station, where it is seen on 13 September 2019.	**Robert Pritchard**

▼ In store since 1988, J15 0-6-0 184 is seen minus its tender in the workshops at RPSI Whitehead on 14 September 2019. 111 J15s were built, mainly in the late 1880s. They were a simple design, so whilst other classes were scrapped and replaced the J15s were repaired and upgraded. 184 joined the RPSI collection in 1977, being restored to appear in a number of films.	**Robert Pritchard**

DUBLIN & SOUTH EASTERN RAILWAY

CLASS K2 — 2-6-0

Built: 1922 by Beyer Peacock & Co, Manchester. Mixed traffic locomotives. 2 built. A regular performer on the main line since 2012, 461 was withdrawn from main line service at the end of 2018 for overhaul.
Boiler Pressure: 175 lbf/sq in.
Cylinders: 19 x 26 in.
Driving Wheel Diameter: 5 ft 1 in.
Weight: 50 tons 1 cwt.

Tractive Effort: 22900 lbf.
Valve Gear: Stephenson.

DSER	GSR/CIÉ				
15	461	MR	RPSI, Whitehead		BP 6112/1922

GREAT SOUTHERN RAILWAYS

CLASS B1a — 4-6-0

Built: 1939 by GSWR for the Dublin–Cork route. This class was the most powerful steam locomotives built for Ireland. 3 built.
Boiler Pressure: 225 lbf/sq in.
Cylinders: (3) 18½ x 28 in.
Driving Wheel Diameter: 6 ft 7 in.
Weight: 84 tons.

Tractive Effort: 34800 lbf.
Valve Gear: Walschaerts.

800	MAEDHBH	M	Ulster Transport Museum, Cultra	Inchicore 1939

7.1.2. Ex-UTA/NIR

LMS (Northern Counties Committee)

CLASS WT — 2-6-4T

Built: 1947 by Derby Locomotive Works, LMS (Ivatt design). 18 built. No. 4 was the last steam locomotive to be used in normal service in Ireland, being withdrawn in 1971. Following overhaul, No. 4 returned to the main line in 2015, often being the RPSI's locomotive based in Dublin.
Boiler Pressure: 200 lbf/sq in.
Cylinders: (O) 19 x 26 in.
Driving Wheel Diameter: 6 ft 0 in.
Weight: 87 tons.

Tractive Effort: 22160 lbf.
Valve Gear: Walschaerts.

4	MM	RPSI, Whitehead	Derby 1947

CLASS U2 — 4-4-0

Built: 1924 by North British Locomotive Co. 18 built (a mixture of new build and rebuilt locomotives).
Boiler Pressure: 170 lbf/sq in.
Cylinders: 19 x 24 in.
Driving Wheel Diameter: 6 ft 0 in.
Weight: 51 tons 10 cwt.

Tractive Effort: 17388 lbf.
Valve Gear: Stephenson.

74	DUNLUCE CASTLE	M	Ulster Transport Museum, Cultra	NBL 2396/1924

BELFAST & COUNTY DOWN RAILWAY

CLASS 1 4-4-2T

Built: 1901 by Beyer Peacock & Co, Manchester. 12 built.
Boiler Pressure: 160 lbf/sq in.   **Tractive Effort:** 14290 lbf.
Cylinders: 17 x 24 in.   **Valve Gear:** Stephenson.
Driving Wheel Diameter: 5 ft 6 in.   **Weight:** 56 tons 18 cwt.

| 30 | 230 | | M | Ulster Transport Museum, Cultra | BP 4231/1901 |

7.1.3. Ex-SLIGO, LEITRIM & NORTHERN COUNTIES RAILWAY

CLASS Z 0-6-4T

Built: 1949 by Beyer Peacock & Co, Manchester. Only originally given a name, not a number. 2 built (these were the last Irish standard gauge steam locomotives built).
Boiler Pressure: 160 lbf/sq in.
Cylinders: 18 x 24 in.
Driving Wheel Diameter: 4 ft 8 in.   **Tractive Effort:** 18890 lbf.
Weight: 54 tons 10 cwt.   **Valve Gear:** Stephenson.

| *SL&NCR* | *NCC/UTA* | | | |
| LOUGH ERNE | 27 | MS | RPSI, Whitehead | BP 7242/1949 |

▲ One of three RPSI locomotives registered for use on the main line at the time of writing, and also fitted with Irish Rail train radios, LMS (Northern Counties Committee) Class WT 2-6-4T "Jeep" No. 4 passes Gormanston with the 13.55 Drogheda–Skerries leg of the RPSI "The Boyne Railtour" on 23 July 2017. **Neil Dinnen**

7.1.4. Ex-GNR(I)/GNRB

CLASS V
4-4-0

Built: 1932 by Beyer Peacock & Co, Manchester. 3-cylinder compound. 5 built for express passenger trains between Dublin and Belfast. Returned to the main line in 2014, its current boiler certificate runs until 2023.
Boiler Pressure: 215 lbf/sq in.
Cylinders: (1 high pressure – inside) 17½ x 26 in. (2 high pressure –outside) 19 x 26 in.
Driving Wheel Diameter: 6 ft 7 in.   **Tractive Effort:** 25245 lbf.
Weight: 65 tons 1 cwt.   **Valve Gear:** Stephenson.

On long-term loan from the Ulster Transport Museum to the RPSI.

| 85 | MERLIN | MM | RPSI, Whitehead | BP 6733/1932 |

CLASS JT
2-4-2T

Built: 1895. 6 built for Dublin suburban services, the class later worked branch line trains.
Cylinders: 16 x 22 in.   **Boiler Pressure:** 175 lbf/sq in.
Driving Wheel Diameter: 5 ft 7 in.   **Tractive Effort:** 13300 lbf.
Weight: 46 tons 2 cwt.   **Valve Gear:** Stephenson.

| 93 | SUTTON | M | Ulster Transport Museum, Cultra | Dundalk 16/1895 |

CLASS Q
4-4-0

Built: 1901 by Neilson Reid, Glasgow. 13 built as mixed traffic locomotives. Returned to the main line in 2017.
Cylinders: 18½ x 26 in.   **Boiler Pressure:** 175 lbf/sq in.
Driving Wheel Diameter: 6 ft 7 in.   **Tractive Effort:** 16755 lbf.
Weight: 49 tons 4 cwt.   **Valve Gear:** Stephenson.

| 131 | URANUS | MM | RPSI, Whitehead | NR 5757/1901 |

▲ GNR Class V 4-4-0 85 "MERLIN" stands at Rosslare Strand with the RPSI "The Sea Breeze" railtour, the 10.40 from Dublin Connolly, on 6 August 2018.   **Finbarr O'Neill**

▲ One of six locos designed and built in-house by the GNR for Dublin and Belfast suburban lines, No. 93 "SUTTON" was used between Dublin, Howth and Malahide when new. On 15 September 2019 it is seen on display at the Ulster Transport Museum, where it has been since 1955 (having been withdrawn four years earlier). **Robert Pritchard**

▼ GNR Class Q 4-4-0 131 "URANUS" is seen in action hauling shuttle trains at RPSI's Whitehead site during a gala weekend on 14 September 2019. **Robert Pritchard**

CLASS S — 4-4-0

Built: 1913 by Beyer Peacock & Co, Manchester. 5 built for express passenger services. Rebuilt 1938 by GNR(I). Undergoing overhaul to main line standards.

Cylinders: 19 x 26 in.	**Boiler Pressure:** 200 lbf/sq in.
Driving Wheel Diameter: 6 ft 7 in.	**Tractive Effort:** 20200 lbf.
Weight: 53 tons 6 cwt.	**Valve Gear:** Stephenson.

171	SLIEVE GULLION	MR	RPSI, Whitehead	BP 5629/1913, rebuilt Dundalk 42/1938

7.2. NARROW GAUGE STEAM LOCOMOTIVES

All locomotives listed below are 3 ft 0 in gauge.

WEST CLARE RAILWAY

CLASS JN1 — 0-6-2T

Built: 1892 by Dübs & Co, Glasgow. 3 built for the West Clare Railway which was the last narrow gauge line with a passenger service, closing in 1961 (despite diesels having been introduced in 1952–53). No. 5 rebuilt 2008–09 by Alan Keef Ltd, Ross-on-Wye for use on the WCR.

Boiler Pressure: 150 lbf/sq in.	**Cylinders:** (O) 15 x 20 in.
Driving Wheel Diameter: 3 ft 6 in.	**Tractive Effort:** 13660 lbf.
Weight: 35 tons 12 cwt.	**Valve Gear:** Stephenson.

WCR		CIÉ			
5	SLIEVE CALLAN	5C	MA	West Clare Railway	Dübs 2890/1892

CAVAN & LEITRIM RAILWAY

CLASS DN2 — 4-4-0T

Built: 1887 by Robert Stephenson & Co. 8 built. Rebuilt with larger boiler 1902–06.

Boiler Pressure: 150 lbf/sq in.	**Cylinders:** (O) 14 x 20 in.
Driving Wheel Diameter: 3 ft 6 in.	**Tractive Effort:** 11900 lbf.
Weight: 26 tons 0 cwt.	**Valve Gear:** Stephenson.

C&LR		CIÉ			
2	KATHLEEN	2L	M	Ulster Transport Museum, Cultra	RS 2613/1887
3	LADY EDITH	3L	M	New Jersey Museum of Transportation, New Jersey, USA	RS 2614/1887

TRALEE & DINGLE RAILWAY

CLASS PN2 — 2-6-2T

Built: 1892 by Hunslet. Transferred to the Cavan & Leitrim Railway in 1949. 1 built.

Boiler Pressure: 150 lbf/sq in.	**Cylinders:** (O) 13½ x 18 in.
Driving Wheel Diameter: 3 ft 0½ in.	**Tractive Effort:** 11620 lbf.
Weight: 39 tons 10 cwt.	**Valve Gear:** Walschaerts.

T&DR		CIÉ			
5		5T	MS	Tralee & Dingle Steam Railway, Blennerville	HE 555/1892

COUNTY DONEGAL RAILWAYS JOINT COMMITTEE

CLASS 5a   2-6-4T

Built: 1912 by Nasmyth, Wilson & Co. 3 built.
Boiler Pressure: 175 lbf/sq in.   **Cylinders:** (O) 15½ x 21 in.
Driving Wheel Diameter: 4 ft 0 in.   **Tractive Effort:** 14300 lbf.
Weight: 50 tons 8 cwt.   **Valve Gear:** Walschaerts.

2	BLANCHE	M	Ulster Transport Museum, Cultra	NW 956/1912

CLASS 5   2-6-4T

Built: 1907 by Nasmyth, Wilson & Co. 5 built.
Boiler Pressure: 175 lbf/sq in.   **Cylinders:** (O) 14 x 21 in.
Driving Wheel Diameter: 4 ft 0 in.   **Tractive Effort:** 12755 lbf.
Weight: 43 tons 10 cwt.   **Valve Gear:** Walschaerts.

16–4	MEENGLASS	P	Foyle Valley Railway Museum, Londonderry	NW 828/1907
17–5	DRUMBOE	MR	RPSI, Whitehead	NW 829/1907
18–6	COLUMBKILLE	M	Foyle Valley Railway Museum, Londonderry	NW 830/1907

PORTSTEWART TRAMWAY

TRAM ENGINES   0-4-0

Built: 1882–83 by Kitson.
Boiler Pressure: 160 lbf/sq in.   **Cylinders:** 8 x 12 in.
Driving Wheel Diameter: 2 ft 4¼ in.   **Tractive Effort:** 3680 lbf.
Weight: 9 tons.   **Valve Gear:** Modified Walschaerts.

1	M	Streetlife Museum of Transport, Hull	K T56/1882
2	M	Ulster Transport Museum, Cultra	K T84/1883

▲ No. 2 "BLANCHE" was one of three of its type built for the newly-formed County Donegal Railways Joint Committee in 1912. Although built to 3 ft gauge it was a powerful loco for its size and was widely used to haul passenger and goods trains across the 121-mile network. It is seen on display at the Ulster Transport Museum at Cultra on 15 September 2019. **Robert Pritchard**

7.3. DIESEL LOCOMOTIVES

Owners of each locomotive are shown in brackets after the location. PO indicates privately owned.

7.3.1. Ex-CIÉ/IRISH RAIL

001 CLASS (ORIGINALLY CLASS A)   Co-Co

Built: 1955–56 by Metropolitan Vickers at Dukinfield Works, Manchester. Rebuilt 1968–71 by CIE at Inchicore Works, Dublin. These locos, formerly known as the "A" Class, were originally fitted with Crossley HST V8 engines of 1200 hp (896 kW). During the conversion process the original electrical equipment was retained, with the main generator being rewound. In their heyday the class were the backbone of the main line passenger and freight services on the CIÉ/IR network and also worked trains into Northern Ireland. The last members of the class were withdrawn in April 1995. 60 built.
Engine: General Motors 12-cylinder 645E, twin bank, two-stroke, blower scavenged, of 990 kW (1325 hp) gross at 800 rpm of which 930 kW (1250 hp) is available for traction.
Transmission: Electric. 6 axle-hung nose-suspended Metropolitan Vickers MV137CW traction motors.
Maximum Tractive Effort: 205 kN (46 000 lbf).
Continuous Tractive Effort: 80 kN (18 000 lbf) at 21.5 mph.
Power At Rail: 750 kW (1013 hp).
Length Over Buffers: 15.54 m (51 ft 0 in)
Train Brakes: Vacuum.

Weight: 82 tons.
Wheel Diameter: 965 mm (3 ft 2 in).
Maximum Speed: 75 mph.

A55 is incorporated into a pub and museum. The pub closed in 2011 but visits to the museum and to view A55 are still available by prior arrangement through the owner Sean Browne. email info@hellskitchenmuseum.com, phone +353 87 230 8152, or see the website www.hellskitchenmuseum.com.

A3	003	S	West Clare Railway (ITG)	MV 889/1955
A15	015	S	West Clare Railway (WCR)	MV 901/1955
A39	039	MA	Downpatrick & County Down Railway (ITG)	MV 925/1956
A55	055	P	Hell's Kitchen museum, Castlerea, Co Roscommon (PO)	MV 941/1956

101 CLASS (ORIGINALLY CLASS B)   A1A-A1A

Built: 1956 by the Birmingham Railway Carriage & Wagon Company at Smethwick. 12 built.
Engine: Sulzer 6LDA28 of 715 kW (960 hp) at 710 rpm.
Transmission: Electric. Four Metropolitan Vickers MV137CW traction motors.
Maximum Tractive Effort: 186 kN (41 800 lbf).
Continuous Tractive Effort: 76 kN (16 900 lbf) at 15 mph.
Power At Rail: 538 kW (721 hp).
Weight: 75.5 tons.
Wheel Diameter: 953 mm (3 ft 1½ in).

Length Over Buffers: 14.53 m (47 ft 8 in).
Maximum Speed: 75 mph.

| B103 | | MS | Irish Traction Group, Carrick-on-Suir (ITG) | BRCW DEL22/1956 |

113 CLASS (ORIGINALLY CLASS C2a)   Bo-Bo

Built: 1950–51 by CIE at Inchicore Works, Dublin. This survivor of a class of two is the oldest surviving main line diesel loco in Ireland, having been CIÉ's first main-line diesel locomotive. The engine was originally rated at 685 kW (915 hp), but was uprated in 1956. 2 built.
Engine: Sulzer 6LDA28 of 715 kW (960 hp) at 710 rpm.
Transmission: Electric. Four Metropolitan Vickers MV137CW traction motors.
Maximum Tractive Effort: 205 kN (46 000 lbf).
Continuous Tractive Effort: 102 kN (23 000 lbf) at 9½ mph.
Power At Rail: 538 kW (721 hp).
Weight: 80 tons.
Wheel Diameter: 1118 mm (3 ft 8 in).

Length Over Buffers: 14.45 m (47 ft 5 in).
Maximum Speed: 55 mph.

Originally fitted with train heating boilers which were removed upon the introduction of steam heating vans.

| 1100 | B113 | M | Ulster Transport Museum, Cultra (IR) | Inchicore 1950 |

▲ 113 Class B113, the oldest surviving main line diesel locomotive in Ireland, is seen at the Ulster Transport Museum at Cultra (where it has been since 2011) on 15 September 2019. **Robert Pritchard**

▼ B 201 Class C231 is seen alongside 141 Class 146 at Downpatrick on the Downpatrick & County Down Railway on 13 October 2019. **Courtesy Downpatrick & County Down Railway/ITG**

B 201 CLASS (ORIGINALLY CLASS C)   Bo-Bo

Built: 1956–58 by Metropolitan Vickers at Dukinfield Works, Manchester with Crossley ESTV8 engine of 410 kW (550 hp). Rebuilt 1969–80 by CIE at Inchicore Works. 34 built.
Engine: General Motors 8 cylinder B645E of 1100 hp (821 kW) at 900 rpm with 776 kW (1040 hp) available for traction.
Transmission: Electric. Four Metropolitan Vickers MV137CW traction motors.
Maximum Tractive Effort: 153 kN (34 440 lbf).
Continuous Tractive Effort: 64 kN (14 500 lbf) at 22.2 mph.
Power At Rail: 630 kW (842 hp).
Weight: 61.5 tons.   **Length Over Buffers:** 12.80 m (42 ft).
Wheel Diameter: 965 mm (3 ft 2 in).   **Maximum Speed:** 75 mph.

C227 carries the number C202.

C226	B226	226	MR	Irish Traction Group, Carrick-on-Suir (ITG)	MV 972/1956
C227	B227	106	S	Don Butler Commercials, Skeard, near Kilmacow,	
				Co Kilkenny (PO)	MV 973/1956
C231	B231	231	MA	Downpatrick & County Down Railway (ITG)	MV 977/1956

421 CLASS (E)   C

Built: 1962 by CIE at Inchicore Works. 14 built.
Engine: Maybach MD220 of 420 hp (313 kW) with 299 kW (400 hp) available for traction.
Transmission: Hydraulic. Mekydro Torque Converter.
Maximum Tractive Effort: 105 kN (23 940 lbf).
Continuous Tractive Effort:
Power At Rail: 266 kW (356 hp).
Weight: 42.8 tons.   **Length Over Buffers:** 9.56 m (31 ft 4¼ in).
Wheel Diameter: 965 mm (3 ft 2 in).   **Maximum Speed:** 25 mph.
Multiple Working: Within class (seldom used except for trials).

E421	421	M	Downpatrick & County Down Railway (DCDR)	Inchicore 1962
E428	428	P	Former Dunsandle Station, Co Galway (PO)	Inchicore 1962
E432	432	MS	Downpatrick & County Down Railway (DCDR)	Inchicore 1963

G601 CLASS   B

Built: 1956 by Deutz, Cologne, West Germany. 3 built.
Engine: Deutz A8L 614 of 97 kW (130 hp).
Transmission: Hydraulic. Voith Chain Drive.
Maximum Tractive Effort:
Continuous Tractive Effort:
Power At Rail:
Weight: 18 tons.   **Length Over Buffers:** 6.30 m (20 ft 8 in).
Wheel Diameter: 950 mm (3 ft 1¼ in).   **Maximum Speed:** 25 mph.

| G601 | | MS | Irish Traction Group, Carrick-on-Suir (ITG) | Deutz 56119/1956 |

G611 CLASS   B

Built: 1962 by Deutz, Cologne, West Germany. 7 built.
Engine: Deutz A8L 714 of 119 kW (160 hp).
Transmission: Hydraulic. Voith chain drive.
Maximum Tractive Effort:
Continuous Tractive Effort:
Power At Rail:
Weight: 22 tons.   **Length Over Buffers:** 6.45 m (21 ft 2 in).
Wheel Diameter: 950 mm (3 ft 1¼ in).   **Maximum Speed:** 25 mph.

All remaining Locomotives of this class were originally sold to the Irish Sugar Company in 1977. G613 was used at Tuam whilst G616 was originally used at the Carlow premises and later moved to Thurles where it joined G611/G615/G617.

G611 and G617 are on loan to the Downpatrick & County Down Railway from the Irish Traction Group.

G611	MS	Downpatrick & County Down Railway (ITG)	Deutz 57225/1962
G613	MR	Downpatrick & County Down Railway (DCDR)	Deutz 57227/1962
G616	MR	Irish Traction Group, Carrick-on-Suir (ITG)	Deutz 57230/1962
G617	MA	Downpatrick & County Down Railway (ITG)	Deutz 57231/1962

121 CLASS   Bo-Bo

Built: 1960 by General Motors, La Grange, Illinois, USA. These are single-cab locos and hauled trains with the cab leading when running singly. Push-pull fitted. 15 built.
Engine: General Motors 8-cylinder 567C, twin bank, blower-scavenged, developing 710 kW (950 hp) at 835 rpm.
Transmission: Electric. 4 axle-hung nose-suspended General Motors D47 traction motors.
Maximum Tractive Effort: 156 kN (35 000 lbf).
Continuous Tractive Effort: 135 kN (30 400 lbf) at 8 mph.
Power At Rail: 530 kW (710 hp).
Weight: 64 tonnes.   **Length Over Buffers:** 12.15 m.
Wheel Diameter: 1016 mm.   **Train Brakes:** Air and vacuum.
Multiple Working: With Classes 071/141/181. **Maximum Speed:** 75 mph.

| B124 | 124 | S | West Clare Railway (ITG) | GM 26274/1960 |
| B134 | 134 | MR | Inchicore Works, Dublin (RPSI) | GM 26284/1960 |

141 CLASS   Bo-Bo

Built: 1962 by General Motors, La Grange, Illinois, USA. This was basically a double-cab version of the 121 Class. 37 built. Five locomotives of this class are still owned by Irish Rail and remain in store at Inchicore Works (see Irish Rail section).
Engine: General Motors 8-cylinder 567C or 645E, twin bank, blower-scavenged, developing 710 kW (950 hp) at 835 rpm.
Transmission: Electric. 4 axle-hung nose-suspended General Motors D57 traction motors.
Maximum Tractive Effort: 156 kN (35 000 lbf).
Continuous Tractive Effort: 135 kN (30 400 lbf) at 8 mph.
Power At Rail: 530 kW (710 hp).
Weight: 67 tonnes.   **Length Over Buffers:** 13.42 m.
Wheel Diameter: 1016 mm.   **Train Brakes:** Air and Vacuum.
Multiple Working: With Classes 071/121/181. **Maximum Speed:** 75 mph.

B141 and B142 are in original 1962 black & tan livery.

B141	141	S	Connolly Depot, Dublin (RPSI)	GM 27467/1962
B142	142	MA	RPSI, Whitehead (RPSI)	GM 27468/1962
B146	146	MA	Downpatrick & County Down Railway (ITG)	GM 27472/1962
B152	152	S	West Clare Railway (ITG)	GM 27478/1962
B175	175	S	Connolly Depot, Dublin (RPSI)	GM 27501/1962

181 CLASS   Bo-Bo

Built: 1966 by General Motors, La Grange, Illinois, USA as a more powerful development of the 141 Class. 12 built.
Engine: General Motors 8-cylinder 645E, twin bank, blower-scavenged, developing 820 kW (1100 hp) at 900 rpm.
Transmission: Electric. 4 axle-hung nose-suspended General Motors D77 traction motors.
Maximum Tractive Effort: 167 kN (37 500 lbf).
Continuous Tractive Effort: 118 kN (26 400 lbf) at 11 mph.
Power At Rail: 605 kW (810 hp).
Weight: 67 tonnes.   **Length Over Buffers:** 13.42 m.
Wheel Diameter: 1016 mm.   **Train Brakes:** Air and Vacuum.
Multiple Working: With Classes 071/121/141. **Maximum Speed:** 75 mph.

| B190 | 190 | S | West Clare Railway (ITG) | GM 31257/1966 |

▲ 101 Class Bo-Bo 102 "FALCON" is seen on display at the Ulster Transport Museum at Cultra on 15 September 2019.
Robert Pritchard

▼ Former County Donegal Railways Joint Committee tractor locomotive No. 11 "PHOENIX" is also seen on display at the Ulster Transport Museum on 15 September 2019. This was originally built as a steam locomotive.
Robert Pritchard

7.3.2. Ex-NORTHERN IRELAND RAILWAYS

1 CLASS   0-6-0

Built: 1969 by English Electric at Vulcan Foundry, Newton-le-Willows.
Engine: Dorman 12QTV of 620 hp (463 kW) at 1800 rpm.
Transmission: Hydraulic. EE Twin Disc DBSG138-2 Torque Converter coupled to a Wiseman 15RLGB1 final drive.
Maximum Tractive Effort: 110 kN (25000 lbf).
Continuous Tractive Effort:
Power At Rail:
Weight: 42.5 tons.
Length Over Buffers: 8.64 m (28 ft 4 in).
Wheel Diameter: 1067 mm (3 ft 6 in).
Maximum Speed: 30 mph.

1		S	Beaver Power Limited, Merthyr Tydfil, South Wales	EEV D1266/1969

101 CLASS   Bo-Bo

Built: 1970 by BR at Doncaster Works, as sub-contractors for The Hunslet Engine Company, Leeds. Push-Pull fitted for operation of NIR stock only.
Engine: English Electric 8CSVT of 1007 kW (1350 hp) at 850 rpm.
Transmission: Electric.
Traction Motors: English Electric 253AZ.
Max. Tractive Effort: 187 kN (42000 lbf).
Cont. Tractive Effort: 112 kN (25200 lbf) at 15 mph.
Power At Rail:
Weight: 68 tons.
Length Over Buffers: 13.77 m.
Wheel Diameter: 1016 mm.
Maximum Speed: 80 mph.

102	FALCON	M	Ulster Transport Museum, Cultra	Doncaster 1970

7.3.3.   Ex-COUNTY DONEGAL RAILWAYS JOINT COMMITTEE

TRACTOR   B

Built: 1928 by Atkinson-Walker for the Clogher Valley Railway. Built as a rail steam tractor. Rebuilt by GNR(I) as a diesel shunter and used by County Donegal Railways from 1932 for shunting and light goods trains.
Engine: Gardner 6L2.
Gauge: 3 ft 0 in.
Transmission: Mechanical.
Weight: 12 tons.
Length over Buffers:
Maximum Speed: 27 mph.

11	PHOENIX	M	Ulster Transport Museum, Cultra	AtW 114 1928

7.4. RAILCARS & RAILBUSES

7.4.1. EX-CIÉ/IRISH RAIL

CIÉ DMSO   1A-A1

Built: 1952 by Park Royal Vehicles, London.
Engine: Two AEC 6-cylinder 9.6 litre, each developing 93 kW (125 hp) at 1800 rpm.
Transmission: Mechanical with Wilson 5-speed epicyclic gearbox.
Accommodation: 12/32 1T.
Weight: 38.5 tons.   **Length:** 20.27 m (66 ft 6 in).
Width: 2.90 m (9 ft 6 in).   **Maximum Speed:** 75 mph.
Converted to loco-hauled push-pull driving trailer by CIÉ at Inchicore Works 1974. Details:
Accommodation: –/58.   **Weight:** 30 tonnes.

DMU No.	Coach No.			
2624	6111	MS	Downpatrick & County Down Railway	PRV 1952

7.4.2. Ex-UTA/NORTHERN IRELAND RAILWAYS

LMS (NORTHERN COUNTIES COMMITTEE)   1A-A1

Built: 1933 by LMS (NCC) at Belfast York Road Works.
Engines: Two Leyland 97 kW (130 hp) petrol. Re-engined 1959 with two Leyland 600 93 kW (125 hp) diesel.
Transmission: Mechanical. Leyland.
Accommodation: 6/55.
Weight: 32 tons.   **Length:** 17.07 m (57 ft 0 in).
Width: 2.95 m (9 ft 8 in).   **Maximum Speed:**

1	MS	RPSI, Whitehead	NCC 1933

RAILBUS   A-A

Built: 1981 by BREL at Derby Carriage & Wagon Works. Designed by BR Research. Originally used as an experimental vehicle on BR. Sold to NIR 1982 and used on the Portrush branch before withdrawal in 1990.
Engine: One Leyland 690 of 150 kW (200 hp).
Transmission: Mechanical. Self Changing Gears.
Accommodation: –/56.
Weight: 19.40 tonnes.   **Length:** 15.30 m (50 ft 2¼ in).
Width: 2.50 m (8 ft 2½ in).   **Maximum Speed:** 75 mph.

BR	NIR			
RDB 977020	RB3	MS	Downpatrick & County Down Railway	BREL Derby 1981

80 CLASS   2-Bo/2-2

Built: 1974–78 by BREL at Derby Carriage & Wagon Works. 8752 rebuilt 1981 from Mark 2C TSO 5516 built 1969. These popular units, nicknamed "Thumpers" were withdrawn by NIR in 2011, although several vehicles continued to be used for Sandite duties until 2017. Generally operated in 2-, 3- or 4-car formation.
Engine: English Electric 4SRKT turbo-charged of 420 kW (560 hp) at 850 rpm.
Traction Motors: Two EE 538 of 220 hp (164 kW).   **Transmission:** Electric.
Accommodation: DMBSO –/42, DTSO –/81 1T (* –/75 1T).
Weight: 62/28 tonnes (* 32.5 tonnes).   **Length:** 20.28/20.38 m.
Width: 2.79 m.   **Maximum Speed:** 70 mph.

▲ Ex-Great Northern Railway Railcar No. 1, originally built as a road bus and later converted to railway use, is seen on display at the Ulster Transport Museum at Cultra on 15 September 2019.

Robert Pritchard

▼ Superbly restored into their original NIR maroon and blue livery, 80 Class set 69+749 is seen at Downpatrick on 13 October 2019.

Courtesy Downpatrick & County Down Railway

NIR Nos.		Type				
69	8069	DMBSO	MA	Downpatrick & County Down Railway	BREL Derby 1978	
90	8090	DMBSO	S	Downpatrick & County Down Railway	BREL Derby 1978	
99	8099	DMBSO	S	East Lancashire Railway	BREL Derby 1977	
749	8749	DTSO	MA	Downpatrick & County Down Railway	BREL Derby 1978	
752	8752	DTSO *	S	Downpatrick & County Down Railway	BREL Derby 1981	
771	8771	DTSO	S	Cherith House, Castle Road, Ballynure, Co Antrim	BREL Derby 1979	

450   "CASTLE CLASS"   2-Bo + 2-2 + 2-2

Built: 1987 by BREL at Derby Carriage & Wagon Works using underframes from condemned BR York-built Mark 1 coaches and engines recovered from former 70 Class units. Nine 3-car units built. Withdrawn by NIR in 2012. At Downpatrick it is often used as either hauled stock or to house a static buffet at Inch Abbey station.
Formation: DMBSO–TSO–DTSO.
Engine: English Electric 4SRKT turbo-charged of 410 kW (550 hp) at 850 rpm.
Traction Motors: Two EE 538 of 220 hp (164 kW).   **Transmission:** Electric.
Accommodation: DMBSO –/38 (+3), TSO –/78 (+7) 1T, DTSO –68 (+7) 1T.
Weight: 62 + 30.4 + 32.4 tonnes.   **Length:** 20.28 + 20.38 +20.28 m.
Width: 2.74 m.   **Maximum Speed:** 70 mph.

NIR Nos.		Type				
458	8458	DMBSO	MA	Downpatrick & County Down Railway	BREL Derby 1987	
798	8798	TSO	MA	Downpatrick & County Down Railway	BREL Derby 1987	
788	8788	DTSO	MA	Downpatrick & County Down Railway	BREL Derby 1987	

7.4.3. Ex-GREAT NORTHERN RAILWAY(I)

GREAT NORTHERN RAILWAY(I)   1A

Built: Built as a petrol road bus in 1928. Converted to rail use in 1934. Converted to a civil engineers vehicle in 1956, it operated until 1963.
Engine: Gardner 4LW of 60 hp.
Transmission: Mechanical.
Accommodation: –/32.
Maximum Speed: 45 mph.

E2	1	8178	M	Ulster Transport Museum, Cultra	GNR(I) 1934

7.4.4. Ex-SLIGO, LEITRIM & NORTHERN COUNTIES RAILWAY

DMBTO   B-2

Built: 1947 by Walker Brothers, Wigan. Bought by CIÉ 1958.
Engine: Gardner 6LW developing 76 kW (102 hp) at 1700 rpm of which 71 kW (96 hp) is available for traction.
Transmission: Mechanical with Wilson 4-speed epicyclic gearbox.
Accommodation: –/59.
Weight: 18.6 tons.   **Length:** 16.75 m (54 ft 11½ in).
Width: 2.90 m (9 ft 6 in).   **Maximum Speed:** 45 mph.

SL&NCR	CIÉ				
B	2509	S	Downpatrick & County Down Railway	WkB 1947	

7.4.5. Ex-COUNTY DONEGAL RAILWAYS JOINT COMMITTEE

RAILCAR   1A

Built: 1906 by Alldays & Onions, Birmingham. The first railway vehicle with an internal combustion engine in Ireland. Built as an open topped railway inspection vehicle, it was given a covered body in 1920.
Engine: 10 hp Petrol. Later re-engined with 22 hp then 36 hp Ford petrol engines.
Transmission: Mechanical.
Accommodation: –/6.
Length: 2.57 m (8 ft 5 in).
Weight: 1 ton 4½ cwt.
Width: 1.09 m (3 ft 7 in).

1		M	Ulster Transport Museum, Cultra	A&O 1906

RAILCAR TRAILER   1A-A1

Built: 1926 by Drewry Car Co Ltd London for Dublin & Blessington Steam Tramway. Rebuilt and regauged by CDR Stranorlar 1934. Rebuilt as a trailer in 1944.
Engine: 35 hp petrol (as built).
Transmission: Mechanical.
Accommodation: –/32.
Length: 8.5 m (27 ft 10 in).
Weight: 4 tons.
Width: 2.13 m (7 ft).

D&BST	CDRJC			
?	3	M	Ulster Transport Museum, Cultra	DC 1926

RAILCAR   B-2

Built: 1932 by Walker Brothers, Wigan for the Clogher Valley Railway. Following the closure of the CVR in 1941 the railcar was bought by the County Donegal Railway in 1942 and operated until 1959.
Engine: Gardner 6L2.
Transmission: Mechanical.
Accommodation: –/29.
Length: 9.7 m (31 ft 10 in).
Weight: 11¾ tons.
Width: 2.13 m (7 ft).

CVR	CDRJC			
1	10	M	Ulster Transport Museum, Cultra	WkB 1932

RAILCAR   B-2

Built: 1934/1940 Walker Brothers, Wigan and GNR(I), Dundalk.
Engine: Gardner 6L2 (* Gardner 6LW of 102 hp).
Transmission: Mechanical.
Accommodation: –/41 (* –/43).
Length: 12.9 m (42 ft 3 in).
Weight: 12 tons.
Width: 2.31 m (7 ft 7 in).

18 is on loan from the North West of Ireland Railway Society.

12	M	Foyle Valley Railway Museum, Londonderry	WkB 1934
18*	MA	Fintown Railway	WkB 1940

RAILCAR   B-2

Built: 1950–51 by Walker Brothers, Wigan and GNR(I), Dundalk. Sold to the Isle of Man Railway in 1961.
Engine: Gardner 6LW of 102 hp.
Transmission: Mechanical with Meadows four-speed gearbox.
Accommodation: –/41.
Weight: 11 tons 5 cwt.
Width: 2.29 m (7 ft 6 in).
Length: 12.57 m (41 ft 2¾ in).
Maximum Speed: 30 mph.

19	S	Douglas Carriage Shed, Isle of Man	WkB 1950
20	S	Douglas Carriage Shed, Isle of Man	WkB 1951

▶ Belfast Corporation tram 249 began life as a horse-drawn tram in the 1890s. In 1905 it was substantially rebuilt and converted to an electric tram, powered by two 35 hp motors mounted on a brill truck. Some 50 original horse trams were converted to electric and numbered 201–250, with 244–250 being open toppers. 249 was withdrawn in 1948 and originally presented to the Belfast Transport Museum in 1955. It is seen at the Ulster Transport Museum at Cultra on 15 September 2019, displayed in the red & cream livery used before 1929. **Robert Pritchard**

▼ Former Dublin United tram No. 224 is seen on display at the National Transport Museum of Ireland at Howth on 14 April 2019. **John Dungey**

7.5. FORMER BR ELECTRIC MULTIPLE UNITS

CLASS 421 (3 Cig)

A peculiarity in this book is former BR Southern Region Cig EMU 1498, which arrived in Ireland in 2016. This was withdrawn by South West Trains in 2010, having spent five years dedicated to the Lymington branch.
Built: 1972 by BREL York for Central Division of BR Southern Region.
Formation: DTCsoL–MBSO–DTCsoL.
Traction Motors: Four EE EE507 of 250 hp (185 kW).   **Accommodation:** DTCsoL 24/28 2T, MBSO –/56.
Weight: 35 + 49 + 35 tonnes.   **Length:** 20.23 + 20.18 +20.23 m.
Width: 2.82 m.   **Maximum Speed:** 90 mph.

BR No.	Type				
62411	MBSO	S	Quirky Nights Glamping Village, Muckduff, Enniscrone, Co Sligo	BREL York 1972
76773	DTCsoL	S	Quirky Nights Glamping Village, Muckduff, Enniscrone, Co Sligo	BREL York 1972
76844	DTCsoL	S	Quirky Nights Glamping Village, Muckduff, Enniscrone, Co Sligo	BREL York 1972

7.6. PRESERVED TRAMS

Preserved electric trams that previously operated in Ireland are listed here.

Tramway and number	Date built	Location
Belfast Corporation No. 249	1905	Ulster Transport Museum, Cultra
Belfast Corporation No. 357	1930	Ulster Transport Museum, Cultra
Bessbrook & Newry No. 2	1885	Ulster Transport Museum, Cultra
Dublin United Director's Car	1901	National Transport Museum of Ireland, Howth
Dublin United No. 224 (replica)	1928	National Transport Museum of Ireland, Howth
Dublin United No. 253	1928	National Transport Museum of Ireland, Howth
Giants Causeway No. 9	1883	National Transport Museum of Ireland, Howth
Hill of Howth No. 2	1900	Orange Empire Railway Museum, Perris, California, USA
Hill of Howth No. 4	1900	Ulster Transport Museum, Cultra
Hill of Howth No. 9	1902	National Transport Museum of Ireland, Howth
Hill of Howth No. 10	1902	National Tramway Museum, Crich, England

▲ In BR Green livery, 3 Cig EMU 1498 is seen after being unloaded at Quirky Nights Glamping Village at Enniscrone on 17 October 2016.   **Neil Dinnen**

8. PRESERVED COACHING STOCK FOR MAIN LINE USE

The Railway Preservation Society of Ireland (RPSI) has a number of coaches for use on main line railtours. These coaches can be split into three distinct fleets, firstly historic coaches (including the Mark 2 State Coach), Cravens coaches (these fleets are based at Inchicore Works or at Heuston Carriage Shed, Dublin) and Mark 2s (based at the RPSI's Whitehead site in Northern Ireland).

8.1. HISTORIC IRISH RAIL COACHES

Most of these vehicles have not been used on the main line since 2010 and are currently stored at Inchicore Works.

GNR(I)   DINING CAR
Built: 1938 by GNR(I) at Dundalk Works.   **Accommodation:** 24/–.
88

GSWR   IRISH PRESIDENT'S STATE COACH
Built: 1902 by GSWR at Inchicore Works.
351

GSWR   COMPARTMENT FIRST
Built: 1921 by GSWR at Inchicore Works.   **Accommodation:** 56/– 2T.
1142

GSWR   COMPARTMENT THIRD
Built: 1936 by GSWR at Inchicore Works.   **Accommodation:** –/56 2T.
1335

CIÉ   OPEN THIRD
Built: 1955 at Inchicore Works using parts supplied by Park Royal, London.
Accommodation: –/70 2T.
1383

CIÉ   OPEN THIRD
Built: 1956 by Park Royal, London. Ran for a time as a snack car, numbered 2423.
Accommodation: –/58 2T.
1419

CIÉ   OPEN THIRD
Built: 1958 at Inchicore Works. Laminate design.
Accommodation: –/64 2T.
1463

CIÉ   BRAKE/GENERATOR SECOND
Built: 1957 at Inchicore Works.   **Accommodation:** –/24 1T.
1916

CIÉ   BUFFET CAR
Built: 1956 at Inchicore Works. Laminate design.   **Accommodation:** –/39.

2421

CIÉ   IRISH PRESIDENT'S STATE COACH
Built: 1972 by BREL at Derby Carriage & Wagon Works to Mark 2D design with finishing carried out by CIÉ at Inchicore Works. Rebuilt 1977 at Inchicore for use by the President of the Republic and other dignitaries on special occasions. Currently on display in the museum at RPSI, Whitehead, on loan from Irish Rail.

5408

8.2. CRAVENS COACHING STOCK
The following Cravens coaches are based at Inchicore Works, Dublin. They are regularly used on RPSI railtours. Coaches are in blue and cream livery except stored 1529, still in orange & black livery. General information for 1505–1541:

Heating System: Steam.   **Brakes:** Vacuum
Bogies: B4.   **Couplers:** Screw.
Length: 19.98 m.   **Width:** 2.90 m.
Gangways: British Standard (WR suspension).   **Weight:** 28.7 tons.
Maximum Speed: 75 mph.

OPEN STANDARD
Built: 1963 by Cravens Ltd, Sheffield. **Accommodation:** –/64 2T.

1505 | 1506

OPEN STANDARD WITH SHOP OR BAR
Built: 1963–64 by Cravens Ltd, Sheffield. Rebuilt at Inchicore Works. 1508 has been fitted with a souvenir shop in the former catering area, 1514 is fitted with a bar for serving drinks and 1522 has been fitted with a snack bar and is used as a dining carriage. **Accommodation:** –/47 2T (* –/28 2T, † –/24 2T).

1508 | 1514   * | 1522   †

OPEN STANDARD
Built: 1964 by CIÉ at Inchicore Works from parts supplied by Cravens Ltd. 1539 is being refurbished as a First Class vehicle. **Accommodation:** –/64 2T.

1523 | 1532 | 1539 | 1541
1529   (S) |

GENERATING STEAM & BRAKE VAN
Rebuilt: 1972 by BREL at Derby Carriage & Wagon Works from BR Mark 1 BSKs originally built 1956/1952 by Gloucester RCW (3173) or BR (3185).
Brakes: Vacuum.   **Bogies:** B5.
Length: 20.45 m.   **Width:** 2.82 m.
Couplers: Screw.   **Gangways:** British Standard (WR suspension).
Maximum Speed: 75 mph.   **Weight:** 37.18 tonnes.

3173 is in maroon livery. 3185 is undergoing overhaul at Inchicore Works.

3173   (21146) | 3185   (34093)

In addition to the two vehicles shown above Irish Rail has converted Generating Steam & Brake Van 3187 to act as a departmental coach (see page 33).

90

8.3. EX-NIR & BR COACHING STOCK

The following vehicles are owned by the RPSI, apart from ex-DBSO 8918 at Downpatrick, which is also listed here for completeness. All are Mark 2s except 462. They are regularly used on RPSI railtours, mainly in Northern Ireland. Fitted with a Central Door Locking system. Livery is dark green with yellow lining apart from the ex-Gatwick Express vehicles still in NIR livery. General information:

Heating System: Pressure ventilated (unless stated).
Bogies: B4.
Length: 20.38 m.
Maximum Speed: 100 mph.

Brakes: Vacuum.
Couplers: Screw.
Width: 2.80 m.

CORRIDOR FIRST

Built: 1968–69 by BR at Derby C&W Works to Mark 2A (13475) or Mark 2B (13487) design.
Accommodation: 42/– 2T.   **Weight:** 33 tonnes.

180   (BR 13475) | 181   (BR 13487, DB 977529)

OPEN STANDARD

Built: 1970 by BR at Derby Carriage & Wagon Works to Mark 2B design for NIR.
Accommodation: –/62 2T.   **Weight:** 32 tonnes.

300   (NIR 934, 822)

OPEN STANDARD

Built: 1966–67 by BR at Derby Carriage & Wagon Works to Mark 2 design for BR.
Accommodation: –/64 2T.   **Weight:** 32.5 tonnes.

301   (BR 5207) | 302   (BR 5135)

OPEN STANDARD

Built: 1972 by BR at Derby Carriage & Wagon Works to Mark 2D design for CIÉ with finishing carried out by CIÉ at Inchicore Works. Air conditioned.
Accommodation: –/64 2T.   **Weight:** 31 tonnes (303) or 32 tonnes (304).

303   (IR 5203) | 304   (IR 5106)

OPEN STANDARD

Built: 1970 by BR at Derby Carriage & Wagon Works to Mark 2B design for NIR.
Accommodation: –/62 2T.   **Weight:** 32 tonnes.

305   (NIR 935, 823) (S)

OPEN BRAKE STANDARD

Built: 1966 by BR at Derby Carriage & Wagon Works to Mark 2 design for BR.
Accommodation: –/31 1T.   **Weight:** 32 tonnes.

460   (BR 9382)

GENERATOR VAN

Built: 1969 by Dundalk Works for CIÉ using parts supplied by Werkspoor, Utrecht, The Netherlands.
Weight: 32 tonnes.

462   (IR 3158)

CORRIDOR BRAKE FIRST

Built: 1966 by BR at Derby Carriage & Wagon Works to Mark 2A design for BR. Fitted with a generator.
Accommodation: 24/– 1T.   **Weight:** 33 tonnes.

463   (BR 14091, 17091)

GRILL/BAR/DINING CAR

Built: 1970 by BR at Derby Carriage & Wagon Works to Mark 2F design for NIR. Air conditioned.
Accommodation: –/22 + bar seats 2T.   **Weight:** 33 tonnes.

547

BRAKE GENERATOR VAN

Built: 1969 by BREL at Derby Carriage & Wagon Works to Mark 2B design. Converted to generator van on sale to NIR, rebuilt for use with ex-Gatwick Express coaches in 2002. Air conditioned.
Accommodation: no seats.   **Weight:** 36 tonnes.

8911 (14104)   (S)   Whitehead

DRIVING BRAKE OPEN STANDARD

Built: 1974 by BREL at Derby Carriage & Wagon Works to Mark 2F design. Converted from BSO at Glasgow in 1985. Converted by LH Group, Barton-under-Needwood to operate as a Driving Trailer with the former Gatwick Express stock but never used in service by NIR. Preserved at Downpatrick in 2014. Air conditioned.
Accommodation: –/31.   **Weight:** 34 tonnes.

8918 (9712, 9534)   Downpatrick & County Down Railway

OPEN STANDARD

Built: 1974 by BREL at Derby Carriage & Wagon Works to Mark 2F design. Converted by BREL Eastleigh 1983–84 for use on Gatwick Express services. These eight coaches were converted by Alstom Glasgow 2001 for NIR (operated in coupled pairs). Withdrawn by NIR in 2009 and stored for some years before being acquired by the RPSI in 2014. Air conditioned.
Accommodation: –/56 2T (*–/52 2T).   **Weight:** 32.5 tonnes.

8941 (6089, 72634) * + 8942 (6098, 72637)   (S) Dundalk
8943 (6082, 72605)   + 8944 (6080, 72609)   (S) Dundalk
8945 (6017, 72626)   + 8948 (6081, 72647) * (S) Whitehead
8946 (5974, 72627)   + 8947 (6078, 72646)   (S) Whitehead

▲ DBSO 8918 is used by the Downpatrick & County Down Railway as a translator with the 450 Class unit 8458. Both are seen at the Inch Abbey terminus on 15 September 2019.   **Robert Pritchard**

9. MUSEUMS & MUSEUM LINES

Preservation in Ireland is mainly the province of voluntary preservation societies, there being no national museum in the Republic of Ireland. However, the large Ulster Transport Museum at Cultra in Northern Ireland covers the railway history of the whole of the country.

The list of museums and museum lines is grouped into counties, arranged in alphabetical order.

9.1. REPUBLIC OF IRELAND

COUNTY CLARE

West Clare Railway

3 ft gauge. The West Clare Railway was the last of Ireland's 3 ft gauge lines to close in 1961. This section of reopened line runs for around 1½ miles north from its base at Moyasta Junction. Under the leadership of local businessman Jackie Whelan the railway has ambitious plans to extend. Permission to extend the railway across the N67 road at Moyasta has delayed these plans, but track has been laid towards Kilkee, and it is hoped that this could be followed by the line to Kilrush. A new 8-road museum is also planned at the Moyasta station site to house the stored Irish Traction Group locomotives and other items of coaching stock, but at the current time these are all in open storage, albeit mostly under tarpaulins.

The railway is open Sunday and Bank Holiday afternoons between May and September, although it is best to check in advance of travel. Original WCR railway steam locomotive No. 5 "Slieve Callan", which was plinthed at Ennis station between 1959 and 1996, returned to action in 2009 after restoration and is used most during most days of operation. There is also a museum telling the history of the railway.

The Moyasta Junction base lies a few miles inland of Kilkee. It is possible to reach Moyasta by bus from Limerick or Ennis although there are only a small number of these each day. Contact: 00353 87 791 9289. www.westclarerailway.ie

COUNTY DONEGAL

Donegal Railway Heritage Centre

County Donegal Railway Restoration CLC, on Tyrconnell Street in Donegal Town, aims to reopen a section of the old County Donegal Railway as a tourist railway with the operation of restored vintage CDR steam and diesel trains.

The museum and shop in the former station at Donegal has displays, pictures and information of the County Donegal and Londonderry & Lough Swilly Railways, that once had 225 miles of 3 ft gauge railway in the County – all of which had closed by 1959. Some former Donegal Railway coaches are exhibited outside.

Open Mondays–Saturdays all year round and Sundays April–September. Contact: 00353 74 972 2655. www.donegalrailway.com

Fintown Railway

3 ft gauge. The Fintown Railway is the only operational railway in County Donegal and runs for around 3 miles from Fintown along the shores of Lough Finn towards Glenties on the trackbed of the County Donegal Glenties branch which closed to passenger traffic in 1947 and to freight five years later. The first section reopened in 1995. A Simplex 102T locomotive is normally used in conjunction with either original County Donegal Railways Railcar No. 18 or a former Shane's Castle Railway bogie carriage for passenger services.

This railway is not accessible by public transport, the nearest major towns being Letterkenny (with buses from Londonderry) or Donegal (buses from Sligo).

Open afternoons during the summer from the start of June to mid September. Also for special events such as Santa specials. Contact: 00353 74 954 6280. www.fintownrailway.com

COUNTY GALWAY

Connemara Railway Revival

Not technically a museum, but this fledgling company is worth a mention. It has been established to reopen a short 400 m section of the Midland Great Western Railway of Ireland Galway–Clifden branch as an operational railway from Maam Cross station. Track laying work was well-advanced during the first half of 2020 with the aim of launching with a 3 ft gauge demonstration or "pop-up" railway, with this being replaced by an Irish standard gauge railway in 2021. The line closed in 1935. Contact: 00353 87 283 2607. www.connemararailway.ie

COUNTY KERRY

Lartigue Monorail

The original Listowel & Ballybunion steam-powered monorail ran for nine miles between Listowel and the resort of Ballybunion along a rail supported on A-shaped trestles. When it opened in 1888 it was the world's first commercial passenger-carrying monorail. The unique line closed in 1924. A section of around one-third of a mile has been recreated at Listowel and a diesel replica of one of the original steam locomotives (built by Alan Keef) is used. There is also a museum where you can learn about the history of the railway.

Operates during the afternoon daily from early May until mid September, at Easter and also the last weekend in September. Buses run from Limerick and Tralee to Listowel. Contact: 00353 68 24393. www.lartiguemonorail.com

▲ The remarkable Lartigue Monorail is well worth a visit. LBR No. 4, a diesel replica of one of the original Lartigue Monorail steam locomotives built by Alan Keef in 2000, is seen at Listowel on 17 May 2017. **Robin Ralston**

COUNTY LAOIS

Stradbally Woodland Railway (Irish Steam Preservation Society)

3 ft gauge. This railway is located in the ground of Stradbally Hall, near Portlaoise. One of the main attractions is the display of traction engines, but there are also steam and diesel locos and a short running line to a "balloon loop" layout, as well as the Stradbally Steam Museum.

The railway runs on Bank Holiday Sunday and Monday afternoons from Easter to October and selected other dates for special events, including a National Steam Rally held in August. Contact: 00353 86 389 0184. www.stradballyrailway.webs.com

COUNTY LEITRIM

Cavan & Leitrim Railway (Dromod)

3 ft gauge. A short (0.75 mile) section of the former Cavan & Leitrim Railway (closed 1959) from Dromod towards Ballinamore has been restored by the Irish Narrow Gauge Trust and trains run three days a week all year round. There are three operational (ex-industrial) locomotives. There is also a transport museum, which includes a large collection of industrial locomotives and rolling stock, as well as aviation, military and motor vehicles. Both the railway and the museum are run by Michael Kennedy.

The railway is located alongside the IR station at Dromod (on the Dublin–Sligo line). Open weekends and Mondays all year. Contact: 00353 71 963 8599. www.cavanandleitrim.com

COUNTY TIPPERARY

Carrick-on-Suir (Irish Traction Group)

A restoration site in the former goods store alongside the Irish Rail station. No public access. The Irish Traction Group is a registered charity and was formed in 1989 with the objective of preserving at least one example of each surviving Irish diesel locomotive class. www.irishtractiongroup.com

COUNTY WATERFORD

Waterford Suir Valley Railway

3 ft gauge. This railway opened in 2002 as a community heritage project and follows the trackbed of the former main line Waterford, Dungarvan & Lismore Railway (closed in 1967). A total of around six miles have been relaid from the station and headquarters of the line at Kilmeadan to Gracedieu Junction and on to Bilberry (trains only normally run over the full length of the line on Saturdays and at special events). A restored LH 348 Simplex locomotive is normally used. Former Irish Rail Mark 2 coach 4106 is used as an office, shop and tearoom at Kilmeadan. There are future plans to extend the line further into Waterford city.

The railway runs daily from April to September and also at the October and February half-terms and at Christmas. Kilmeadan is around seven miles from Waterford and is served by local buses (25 minute walk to the railway). Contact: 00353 051 384 058. www.wsvrailway.ie

Closed lines:
The 3 ft Tralee & Dingle Steam Railway in County Kerry has not operated trains since the summer 2009 season, although there have been attempts at reopening, but the steam locomotive used (No. 5) is in need of a major overhaul. The Bord na Móna-operated Clonmacnoise & West Offaly Railway closed in 2008 and Bord na Móna now no longer operate any heritage lines.

9.2. NORTHERN IRELAND

COUNTY ANTRIM

Giant's Causeway & Bushmills Railway

3 ft gauge. This railway reopened in 2002 using some locomotives and rolling stock which were once used at Shane's Castle Railway (closed in 1994), including a Peckett 0-4-0WT built in 1904 for the British Aluminium Company. Delivered in 2010 was a purpose-built 4-car tram-style DMU built by Severn Lamb UK and designed as a replica of the former trains used on the line. The line runs for two miles from Bushmills village north along the coast to the Giant's Causeway World Heritage Site along the trackbed of the former Giant's Causeway, Portrush & Bush Valley Railway & Tramway Company line from Portrush to the Giants Causeway, which closed in 1949.

Operates on Fridays, Saturdays and Sundays March–October and daily in July and August. Contact: 028 2073 2844. www.freewebs.com/giantscausewayrailway

Railway Preservation Society of Ireland, Whitehead

The RPSI's headquarters at Whitehead, just past the Belfast–Larne line station, is principally a restoration site and also hosts a number open weekends every year. Recent years has seen significant investment in a new museum. The Society was formed in 1964 to preserve Irish steam locomotives, carriages and other rolling stock and operate them on the main line, in close collaboration with Irish Rail and NIR. It runs around 90 main line trips a year across the country, many of which start from Whitehead excursion platform. The RPSI also has a second restoration site at Mullingar, Co Westmeath. Contact: 028 9358 6200. www.steamtrainsireland.com

COUNTY DOWN

Ulster Transport Museum, Cultra

This excellent museum has separate sections for railways, trams, cars and ships and describes its collection as one of the most comprehensive in Europe. It also has a miniature railway, but the connection to the main line is long-disused. The museum is open all year round (apart from Mondays that are not Bank Holidays). It is located a short walk from Cultra station, on the Belfast–Bangor line. Adjacent is the separate Ulster Folk Museum. Contact: 028 9042 8428. www.nmni.com/utm

Downpatrick & County Down Railway

This is the only Irish standard gauge preserved railway in Ireland. Laid on the formation of the former Belfast & County Down Railway (closed 1950) the railway has around 3½ miles of track: 2½ miles from Downpatrick to a new station built at Inch Abbey (the normal running line) and around one mile on the former route to Newcastle. The DCDR was established in 1985 with the aim of restoring a portion of the former B&CDR as a working railway museum. The next step is to extend along the former B&CDR Ardglass branch to Ballydugan.

The railway has developed a reputation for holding a series of excellent events every year, including diesel galas. It operates every weekend afternoon from mid June to mid September and other selected weekends throughout the year for special events. Various bus routes operate to Downpatrick, including direct from Belfast, and the bus station is adjacent to the railway station. Contact: 028 4461 5779. www.downrail.co.uk

COUNTY LONDONDERRY

Foyle Valley Railway Museum, Londonderry

This museum reopened under new owners in 2016. Now operated by Destined Ltd, a charity for adults with learning disabilities. The site was formerly the Foyle Road terminus of the Great Northern Railway (I). A section of 3 ft track had been laid on the former GNR(I) formation but this is now disused. Steam locomotive No. 4 was cosmetically restored at Whitehead and returned to the museum for display outside in 2019. The museum includes a visitor centre and cafe. Listed opening dates at the time of writing are Tuesdays–Saturdays in June–August. Contact: 028 7136 2424. www.destined.ie

As well as the railways listed above there are a number of narrow gauge industrial railways in Ireland. These are mainly the Bord na Móna peat railways which operate across the middle of the country. Most are 3 ft gauge. For details of operating passenger narrow gauge and miniature railways in Ireland see the Platform 5 publication "Miniature Railways of Great Britain & Ireland".

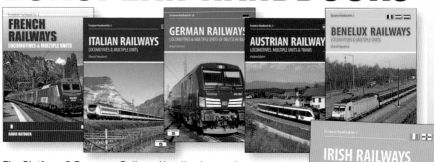